William Shakespeare's

Othello

Text by
Michael A. Modugno
(B.A., Rutgers University)
Department of English
Piscataway High School
Piscataway, New Jersey

Illustrations by
Karen Pica

 Research & Education Association

MAXnotes® for
OTHELLO

Printed in the United States of America

Library of Congress Catalog Card Number 00-130592

International Standard Book Number 0-87891-038-7

MAXnotes® is a registered trademark of
Research & Education Association, Piscataway, New Jersey 08854

What **MAXnotes®** Will Do for You

This book is intended to help you absorb the essential contents and features of William Shakespeare's *Othello* and to help you gain a thorough understanding of the work. Our book has been designed to do this more quickly and effectively than any other study guide.

For best results, this **MAXnotes** book should be used as a companion to the actual work, not instead of it. The interaction between the two will greatly benefit you.

To help you in your studies, this book presents the most up-to-date interpretations of every section of the actual work, followed by questions and fully explained answers that will enable you to analyze the material critically. The questions also will help you to test your understanding of the work and will prepare you for discussions and exams.

Meaningful illustrations are included to further enhance your understanding and enjoyment of the literary work. The illustrations are designed to place you into the mood and spirit of the work's settings.

The **MAXnotes** also include summaries, character lists, explanations of plot, and section-by-section analyses. A biography of the author and discussion of the work's historical context will help you put this literary piece into the proper perspective of what is taking place.

The use of this study guide will save you the hours of preparation time that would ordinarily be required to arrive at a complete grasp of this work of literature. You will be well prepared for classroom discussions, homework, and exams. The guidelines that are included for writing papers and reports on various topics will prepare you for any added work which may be assigned.

The **MAXnotes** will take your grades "to the max."

Dr. Max Fogiel
Program Director

Contents

Each Scene includes a List of Characters, Summary, Analysis, Study Questions and Answers, and Suggested Essay Topics.

MAXnotes® are simply the best – but don't just take our word for it...

"... I have told every bookstore in the area to carry your MAXnotes. They are the only notes I recommend to my students. There is no comparison between MAXnotes and all other notes ..."

– High School Teacher & Reading Specialist,
Arlington High School, Arlington, MA

"... I discovered the MAXnotes when a friend loaned me her copy of the *MAXnotes for Romeo and Juliet.* The book really helped me understand the story. Please send me a list of stores in my area that carry the MAXnotes. I would like to use more of them ..."

– Student, San Marino, CA

A Glance at Some of the Characters

Othello

Desdemona

Iago

Cassio

Brabantio

Emilia

Roderigo

Duke of Venice

Introduction

The Life and Work of William Shakespeare

The details of William Shakespeare's life are sketchy, mostly mere surmise based upon court or other clerical records. His parents, John and Mary (Arden), were married about 1557; she was of the landed gentry, and he was a yeoman—a glover and commodities merchant. By 1568, John had risen through the ranks of town government and held the position of high bailiff, which was a position similar to mayor. William, the eldest son and the third of eight children, was born in 1564, probably on April 23, several days before his baptism on April 26 in Stratford-upon-Avon. Shakespeare is also believed to have died on the same date—April 23—in 1616. It is believed that William attended the local grammar school in Stratford where his parents lived, and that he studied primarily Latin, rhetoric, logic, and literature. Shakespeare probably left school at age 15, which was the norm, to take a job, especially since this was the period of his father's financial difficulty. At age 18 (1582), William married Anne Hathaway, a local farmer's daughter who was eight years his senior. Their first daughter (Susanna) was born six months later (1583), and twins Judith and Hamnet were born in 1585.

Shakespeare's life can be divided into three periods: the first 20 years in Stratford, which include his schooling, early marriage, and fatherhood; the next 25 years as an actor and playwright in London; and the last five in retirement in Stratford where he enjoyed moderate wealth gained from his theatrical successes. The years linking the first two periods are marked by a lack of information about Shakespeare, and are often referred to as the "dark years."

At some point during the "dark years," Shakespeare began his career with a London theatrical company, perhaps in 1589, for he was already an actor and playwright of some note by 1592. Shakespeare apparently wrote and acted for numerous theatrical companies, including Pembroke's Men, and Strange's Men, which later became the Chamberlain's Men, with whom he remained for the rest of his career.

In 1592, the Plague closed the theaters for about two years, and Shakespeare turned to writing book-length narrative poetry. Most notable were *Venus and Adonis* and *The Rape of Lucrece*, both of which were dedicated to the Earl of Southampton, whom scholars accept as Shakespeare's friend and benefactor despite a lack of documentation. During this same period, Shakespeare was writing his sonnets, which are more likely signs of the time's fashion rather than actual love poems detailing any particular relationship. He returned to playwriting when theaters reopened in 1594, and did not continue to write poetry. His sonnets were published without his consent in 1609, shortly before his retirement.

Amid all of his success, Shakespeare suffered the loss of his only son, Hamnet, who died in 1596 at the age of 11. But Shakespeare's career continued unabated, and in London in 1599, he became one of the partners in the new Globe Theater, which was built by the Chamberlain's Men.

Shakespeare wrote very little after 1612, which was the year he completed *Henry VIII*. It was during a performance of this play in 1613 that the Globe caught fire and burned to the ground. Sometime between 1610 and 1613, Shakespeare returned to Stratford, where he owned a large house and property, to spend his remaining years with his family.

William Shakespeare died on April 23, 1616, and was buried two days later in the chancel of Holy Trinity Church, where he had been baptized exactly 52 years earlier. His literary legacy included 37 plays, 154 sonnets, and five major poems.

Incredibly, most of Shakespeare's plays had never been published in anything except pamphlet form, and were simply extant as acting scripts stored at the Globe. Theater scripts were not regarded as literary works of art, but only the basis for the performance. Plays were simply a popular form of entertainment for all layers of society in Shakespeare's time. Only the efforts of two of Shakespeare's company, John Heminges and Henry Condell, preserved his 36 plays (minus *Pericles*, the thirty-seventh).

Shakespeare's Language

Shakespeare's language can create a strong pang of intimidation, even fear, in a large number of modern-day readers. Fortunately, however, this need not be the case. All that is needed to master the art of reading Shakespeare is to practice the techniques of unraveling uncommonly-structured sentences and to become familiar with the poetic use of uncommon words. We must realize that during the 400-year span between Shakespeare's time and our own, both the way we live and speak has changed. Although most of his vocabulary is in use today, some of it is obsolete, and what may be most confusing is that some of his words are used today, but with slightly different or totally different meanings. On the stage, actors readily dissolve these language stumbling blocks. They study Shakespeare's dialogue and express it dramatically in word and in action so that its meaning is graphically enacted. If the reader studies Shakespeare's lines as an actor does, looking up and reflecting upon the meaning of unfamiliar words until real voice is discovered, he or she will suddenly experience the excitement, the depth, and the sheer poetry of what these characters say.

Shakespeare's Sentences

In English, or any other language, the meaning of a sentence greatly depends upon where each word is placed in that sentence. "The child hurt the mother" and "The mother hurt the child" have opposite meanings, even though the words are the same, simply because the words are arranged differently. Because word position is so integral to English, the reader will find unfamiliar word arrangements confusing, even difficult to understand. Since Shakespeare's plays are poetic dramas, he often shifts from average word arrangements to the strikingly unusual so that the line will conform to the desired poetic rhythm. Often, too, Shakespeare employs unusual word order to afford a character his own specific style of speaking.

Today, English sentence structure follows a sequence of subject first, verb second, and an optional object third. Shakespeare, however, often places the verb before the subject, which reads, "Speaks he" rather than "He speaks." Solanio speaks with this inverted structure in *The Merchant of Venice* stating, "I should be still/ Plucking the grass to know where sits the wind" (Bevington edition, I, i, ll.17-19), while today's standard English word order would have the clause at the end of this line read, "where the wind sits." "Wind" is the subject of this clause, and "sits" is the verb. Bassanio's words in Act Two also exemplify this inversion: "And in such eyes as ours appear not faults" (II, ii, l. 184). In our normal word order, we would say, "Faults do not appear in eyes such as ours," with "faults" as the subject in both Shakespeare's word order and ours.

Inversions like these are not troublesome, but when Shakespeare positions the predicate adjective or the object before the subject and verb, we are sometimes surprised. For example, rather than "I saw him," Shakespeare may use a structure such as "Him I saw." Similarly, "Cold the morning is" would be used for our "The morning is cold." Lady Macbeth demonstrates this inversion as she speaks of her husband: "Glamis thou art, and Cawdor, and shalt be/What thou art promised" (*Macbeth*, I, v, ll. 14-15). In current English word order, this quote would begin, "Thou art Glamis, and Cawdor."

In addition to inversions, Shakespeare purposefully keeps words apart that we generally keep together. To illustrate, consider Bassanio's humble admission in *The Merchant of Venice*: "I owe you much, and, like a wilful youth,/That which I owe is lost" (I, i, ll. 146-147). The phrase, "like a wilful youth," separates the regular sequence of "I owe you much" and "That which I owe is lost." To understand more clearly this type of passage, the reader could re-arrange these word groups into our conventional order: I owe you much and I wasted what you gave me because I was young and impulsive. While these rearranged clauses will sound like normal English, and will be simpler to understand, they will no longer have the desired poetic rhythm, and the emphasis will now be on the wrong words.

As we read Shakespeare, we will find words that are separated by long, interruptive statements. Often subjects are separated from verbs, and verbs are separated from objects. These long interruptions can be used to give a character dimension or to add an element of suspense. For example, in *Romeo and Juliet* Benvolio describes both Romeo's moodiness and his own sensitive and thoughtful nature:

> I, measuring his affections by my own,
> Which then most sought, where most might not be found,
> Being one too many by my weary self,
> Pursu'd my humour, not pursuing his,
> And gladly shunn'd who gladly fled from me.
> (I, i, ll. 126-130)

In this passage, the subject "I" is distanced from its verb "Pursu'd." The long interruption serves to provide information which is integral to the plot. Another example, taken from *Hamlet*, is the ghost, Hamlet's father, who describes Hamlet's uncle, Claudius, as

> ...that incestuous, that adulterate beast,
> With witchcraft of his wit, with traitorous gifts—
> O wicked wit and gifts, that have the power
> So to seduce—won to his shameful lust
> The will of my most seeming virtuous queen.
> (I, v, ll. 43-47)

From this we learn that Prince Hamlet's mother is the victim of an evil seduction and deception. The delay between the subject, "beast," and the verb, "won," creates a moment of tension filled with the image of a cunning predator waiting for the right moment to spring into attack. This interruptive passage allows the play to unfold crucial information and thus to build the tension necessary to produce a riveting drama.

While at times these long delays are merely for decorative purposes, they are often used to narrate a particular situation or to enhance character development. As *Antony and Cleopatra* opens, an interruptive passage occurs in the first few lines. Although the delay is not lengthy, Philo's words vividly portray Antony's military prowess while they also reveal the immediate concern of the drama.

Antony is distracted from his career and is now focused on
Cleopatra:

> ...those goodly eyes,
> That o'er the files and musters of the war
> Have glow'd like plated Mars, now bend, now turn
> The office and devotion of their view
> Upon a tawny front.... (I, i, ll. 2-6)

Whereas Shakespeare sometimes heaps detail upon detail, his
sentences are often elliptical, that is, they omit words we expect in
written English sentences. In fact, we often do this in our spoken
conversations. For instance, we say, "You see that?" when we really
mean, "Did you see that?" Reading poetry or listening to lyrics in
music conditions us to supply the omitted words and it makes us
more comfortable reading this type of dialogue. Consider one passage in *The Merchant of Venice* where Antonio's friends ask him why
he seems so sad and Solanio tells Antonio, "Why, then you are in
love" (I, i, l. 46). When Antonio denies this, Solanio responds, "Not
in love neither?" (I, i, l. 47). The word "you" is omitted but under-
stood despite the confusing double negative.

In addition to leaving out words, Shakespeare often uses intentionally vague language, a strategy which taxes the reader's attentiveness. In *Antony and Cleopatra*, Cleopatra, upset that Antony
is leaving for Rome after learning that his wife died in battle, convinces him to stay in Egypt:

> Sir, you and I must part, but that's not it:
> Sir you and I have lov'd, but there's not it;
> That you know well, something it is I would—
> O, my oblivion is a very Antony,
> And I am all forgotten.
> (I, iii, ll. 87-91, emphasis added)

In line 89, "...something it is I would" suggests that there is
something that she would want to say, do, or have done. The in-
tentional vagueness leaves us, and certainly Antony, to wonder.
Though this sort of writing may appear lackadaisical for all that it

leaves out, here the vagueness functions to portray Cleopatra as rhetorically sophisticated. Similarly, when asked what thing a crocodile is (meaning Antony himself who is being compared to a crocodile), Antony slyly evades the question by giving a vague reply:

> It is shap'd, sir, like itself, and it is as broad as it hath
> breadth. It is just so high as it is, and moves with it own
> organs. It lives by that which nourisheth it, and, the
> elements once out of it, it transmigrates.
> (II, vii, ll. 43-46)

This kind of evasiveness, or double-talk, occurs often in Shakespeare's writing and requires extra patience on the part of the reader.

Shakespeare's Words

As we read Shakespeare's plays, we will encounter uncommon words. Many of these words are not in use today. As *Romeo and Juliet* opens, we notice words like "shrift" (confession) and "holidame" (a holy relic). Words like these should be explained in notes to the text. Shakespeare also employs words which we still use, though with different meaning. For example, in *The Merchant of Venice* "caskets" refer to small, decorative chests for holding jewels. However, modern readers may think of a large cask instead of the smaller, diminutive casket.

Another trouble modern readers will have with Shakespeare's English is with words that are still in use today, but which mean something different in Elizabethan use. In *The Merchant of Venice*, Shakespeare uses the word "straight" (as in "straight away") where we would say "immediately." Here, the modern reader is unlikely to carry away the wrong message, however, since the modern meaning will simply make no sense. In this case, textual notes will clarify a phrase's meaning. To cite another example, in *Romeo and Juliet*, after Mercutio dies, Romeo states that the "black fate on moe days doth depend" (emphasis added). In this case, "depend" really means "impend."

Shakespeare's Wordplay

All of Shakespeare's works exhibit his mastery of playing with language and with such variety that many people have authored entire books on this subject alone. Shakespeare's most frequently used types of wordplay are common: metaphors, similes, synecdoche and metonymy, personification, allusion, and puns. It is when Shakespeare violates the normal use of these devices, or rhetorical figures, that the language becomes confusing.

A metaphor is a comparison in which an object or idea is replaced by another object or idea with common attributes. For example, in *Macbeth* a murderer tells Macbeth that Banquo has been murdered, as directed, but that his son, Fleance, escaped, having witnessed his father's murder. Fleance, now a threat to Macbeth, is described as a serpent:

> There the grown serpent lies, the worm that's fled
> Hath nature that in time will venom breed,
> No teeth for the present. (III, iv, ll. 29-31, emphasis added)

Similes, on the other hand, compare objects or ideas while using the words "like" or "as." In *Romeo and Juliet,* Romeo tells Juliet that "Love goes toward love as schoolboys from their books" (II, ii, l. 156). Such similes often give way to more involved comparisons, "extended similes." For example, Juliet tells Romeo:

> 'Tis almost morning, I would have thee gone,
> And yet no farther than a wonton's bird,
> That lets it hop a little from his hand
> Like a poor prisoner in his twisted gyves,
> And with silken thread plucks it back again,
> So loving-jealous of his liberty.
> (II, ii, ll. 176-181, emphasis added)

An epic simile, a device borrowed from heroic poetry, is an extended simile that builds into an even more elaborate comparison. In *Macbeth,* Macbeth describes King Duncan's virtues with an angelic, celestial simile and then drives immediately into another simile that redirects us into a vision of warfare and destruction:

> ...Besides this Duncan
> Hath borne his faculties so meek, hath been
> So clear in his great office, that his virtues
> Will plead like angels, trumpet-tongued, against
> The deep damnation of his taking-off;
> And pity, like a naked new-born babe,
> Striding the blast, or heaven's cherubim, horsed
> Upon the sightless couriers of the air,
> Shall blow the horrid deed in every eye,
> That tears shall drown the wind....
> (I, vii, ll. 16-25, emphasis added)

Shakespeare employs other devices, like synecdoche and metonymy, to achieve "verbal economy," or using one or two words to express more than one thought. Synecdoche is a figure of speech using a part for the whole. An example of synecdoche is using the word boards to imply a stage. Boards are only a small part of the materials that make up a stage, however, the term boards has become a colloquial synonym for stage. Metonymy is a figure of speech using the name of one thing for that of another which it is associated. An example of metonymy is using crown to mean the king (as used in the sentence "These lands belong to the crown"). Since a crown is associated with or an attribute of the king, the word crown has become a metonymy for the king. It is important to understand that every metonymy is a synecdoche, but not every synecdoche is a metonymy. This rule is true because a metonymy must not only be a part of the root word, making a synecdoche, but also be a unique attribute of or associated with the root word.

Synecdoche and metonymy in Shakespeare's works is often very confusing to a new student because he creates uses for words that they usually do not perform. This technique is often complicated and yet very subtle, which makes it difficult for a new student to dissect and understand. An example of these devices in one of Shakespeare's plays can be found in *The Merchant of Venice*. In warning his daughter, Jessica, to ignore the Christian revelries in the streets below, Shylock says:

> Lock up my doors; and when you hear the drum
> And the vile squealing of the wry-necked fife,
> Clamber not you up to the casements then...
> (I, v, ll. 30-32)

The phrase of importance in this quote is "the wry-necked fife." When a reader examines this phrase it does not seem to make sense; a fife is a cylinder-shaped instrument, there is no part of it that can be called a neck. The phrase then must be taken to refer to the fife-player, who has to twist his or her neck to play the fife. Fife, therefore, is a synecdoche for fife-player, much as boards is for stage. The trouble with understanding this phrase is that "vile squealing" logically refers to the sound of the fife, not the fife-player, and the reader might be led to take fife as the instrument because of the parallel reference to "drum" in the previous line. The best solution to this quandary is that Shakespeare uses the word fife to refer to both the instrument and the player. Both the player and the instrument are needed to complete the wordplay in this phrase, which, though difficult to understand to new readers, cannot be seen as a flaw since Shakespeare manages to convey two meanings with one word. This remarkable example of synecdoche illuminates Shakespeare's mastery of "verbal economy."

Shakespeare also uses vivid and imagistic wordplay through personification, in which human capacities and behaviors are attributed to inanimate objects. Bassanio, in *The Merchant of Venice*, almost speechless when Portia promises to marry him and share all her worldly wealth, states "my blood speaks to you in my veins..." (III, ii, l. 176). How deeply he must feel since even his blood can speak. Similarly, Portia, learning of the penalty that Antonio must pay for defaulting on his debt, tells Salerio, "There are some shrewd contents in yond same paper / That steals the color from Bassanio's cheek" (III, ii, ll. 243-244).

Another important facet of Shakespeare's rhetorical repertoire is his use of allusion. An allusion is a reference to another author or to an historical figure or event. Very often Shakespeare alludes to the heroes and heroines of Ovid's *Metamorphoses*. For example, in Cymbeline an entire room is decorated with images illustrating the stories from this classical work, and the heroine, Imogen, has been reading from this text. Similarly, in *Titus Andronicus* characters not only read directly from the *Metamorphoses*, but a subplot re-enacts one of the *Metamorphoses's* most famous stories, the rape and mutilation of Philomel.

Another way Shakespeare uses allusion is to drop names of mythological, historical, and literary figures. In *The Taming of the Shrew*, for instance, Petruchio compares Katharina, the woman whom he is courting, to Diana (II, i, l. 55), the virgin goddess, in order to suggest that Katharina is a man-hater. At times, Shakespeare will allude to well-known figures without so much as mentioning their names. In *Twelfth Night*, for example, though the Duke and Valentine are ostensibly interested in Olivia, a rich countess, Shakespeare asks his audience to compare the Duke's emotional turmoil to the plight of Acteon, whom the goddess Diana transforms into a deer to be hunted and killed by Acteon's own dogs:

Duke: That instant was I turn'd into a hart,
                And my desires, like fell and cruel hounds,
                E'er since pursue me.
                [...]
Valentine: But like a cloistress she will veiled walk,
                And water once a day her chamber round....
                (I, i, l. 20 ff.)

Shakespeare's use of puns spotlights his exceptional wit. His comedies in particular are loaded with puns, usually of a sexual nature. Puns work through the ambiguity that results when multiple senses of a word are evoked; homophones often cause this sort of ambiguity. In *Antony and Cleopatra*, Enobarbus believes "there is mettle in death" (I, ii, l. 146), meaning that there is "courage" in death; at the same time, mettle suggests the homophone metal, referring to swords made of metal causing death. In early editions of Shakespeare's work there was no distinction made between the two words. Antony puns on the word "earing," (I, ii, ll. 112-114) meaning both plowing (as in rooting out weeds) and hearing: he angrily sends away a messenger, not wishing to hear the message from his wife, Fulvia: "...O then we bring forth weeds,/

when our quick minds lie still, and our ills told us/Is as our earing." If ill-natured news is planted in one's "hearing," it will render an "earing" (harvest) of ill-natured thoughts. A particularly clever pun, also in *Antony and Cleopatra,* stands out after Antony's troops have fought Octavius's men in Egypt: "We have beat him to his camp. Run one before,/And let the queen know of our gests" (IV, viii, ll. 1-2). Here "gests" means deeds (in this case, deeds of battle); it is also a pun on "guests," as though Octavius' slain soldiers were to be guests when buried in Egypt.

One should note that Elizabethan pronunciation was in several cases different from our own. Thus, modern readers, especially Americans, will miss out on the many puns based on homophones. The textual notes will point out many of these "lost" puns, however.

Shakespeare's sexual innuendoes can be either clever or tedious depending upon the speaker and situation. The modern reader should recall that sexuality in Shakespeare's time was far more complex than in ours and that characters may refer to such things as masturbation and homosexual activity. Textual notes in some editions will point out these puns but rarely explain them. An example of a sexual pun or innuendo can be found in *The Merchant of Venice* when Portia and Nerissa are discussing Portia's past suitors using innuendo to tell of their sexual prowess:

> Portia: I pray thee, overname them, and as thou
>   namest them, I will describe them, and
>   according to my description level at my
>   affection.
> Nerissa: First, there is the Neapolitan prince.
> Portia: Ay, that's a colt indeed, for he doth nothing but
>   talk of his horse, and he makes it a great
>   appropriation to his own good parts that he can
>   shoe him himself. I am much afeard my lady his
>   mother played false with the smith.
>   (I, ii, ll. 35-45)

The "Neapolitan prince" is given a grade of an inexperienced youth when Portia describes him as a "colt." The prince is thought to be inexperienced because he did nothing but "talk of his horse" (a pun for his penis) and his other great attributes. Portia goes on to say that the prince boasted that he could "shoe him [his horse] himself," a possible pun meaning that the prince was very proud that he could masturbate. Finally, Portia makes an attack upon the prince's mother, saying that "my lady his mother played false with the smith," a pun to say his mother must have committed adultery with a blacksmith to give birth to such a vulgar man having an obsession with "shoeing his horse."

It is worth mentioning that Shakespeare gives the reader hints when his characters might be using puns and innuendoes. In *The Merchant of Venice*, Portia's lines are given in prose when she is joking, or engaged in bawdy conversations. Later on the reader will notice that Portia's lines are rhymed in poetry, such as when she is talking in court or to Bassanio. This is Shakespeare's way of letting the reader know when Portia is jesting and when she is serious.

Shakespeare's Dramatic Verse

Finally, the reader will notice that some lines are actually rhymed verse while others are in verse without rhyme; and much of Shakespeare's drama is in prose. Shakespeare usually has his lovers speak in the language of love poetry which uses rhymed couplets. The archetypal example of this comes, of course, from *Romeo and Juliet*:

> The grey-ey'd morn smiles on the frowning night,
> Check'ring the eastern clouds with streaks of light,
> And fleckled darkness like a drunkard reels
> From forth day's path and Titan's fiery wheels.
> (II, iii, ll. 1-4)

Here it is ironic that Friar Lawrence should speak these lines since he is not the one in love. He, therefore, appears buffoonish and out of touch with reality. Shakespeare often has his characters speak in rhymed verse to let the reader know that the character is acting in jest, and vice-versa.

Perhaps the majority of Shakespeare's lines are in blank verse, a form of poetry which does not use rhyme (hence the name blank) but still employs a rhythm native to the English language, iambic pentameter, where every second syllable in a line of ten syllables receives stress. Consider the following verses from *Hamlet*, and note the accents and the lack of end-rhyme:

> The síngle ánd pecúliar lífe is bóund
> With áll the stréngth and ármor óf the mínd
> (III, iii, ll. 12-13)

The final syllable of these verses receives stress and is said to have a hard, or "strong," ending. A soft ending, also said to be "weak," receives no stress. In *The Tempest*, Shakespeare uses a soft ending to shape a verse that demonstrates through both sound (meter) and sense the capacity of the feminine to propagate:

> and thén I lóv'd thee
> And shów'd thee áll the quálitíes o' th' ísle,
> The frésh spríngs, bríne-pits, bárren pláce and fértile.
> (I, ii, ll. 338-40)

The first and third of these lines here have soft endings.

In general, Shakespeare saves blank verse for his characters of noble birth. Therefore, it is significant when his lofty characters speak in prose. Prose holds a special place in Shakespeare's dialogues; he uses it to represent the speech habits of the common people. Not only do lowly servants and common citizens speak in prose, but important, lower class figures also use this fun, at times ribald variety of speech. Though Shakespeare crafts some very ornate lines in verse, his prose can be equally daunting, for some of his characters may speechify and break into double-talk in their attempts to show sophistication. A clever instance of this comes when the Third Citizen in *Coriolanus* refers to the people's paradoxical lack of power when they must elect Coriolanus as their new leader once Coriolanus has orated how he has courageously fought for them in battle:

> We have power in ourselves to do it, but it is
> a power that we have no power to do; for if he show us his
> wounds and tell us his deeds, we are to put our tongues into

those wounds and speak for them; so, if he tell us his noble deeds, we must also tell him our noble acceptance of them. Ingratitude is monstrous, and for the multitude to be ingrateful were to make a monster of the multitude, of the which we, being members, should bring ourselves to be monstrous members.
(II, ii, ll. 3-13)

Notice that this passage contains as many metaphors, hideous though they be, as any other passage in Shakespeare's dramatic verse.

When reading Shakespeare, paying attention to characters who suddenly break into rhymed verse, or who slip into prose after speaking in blank verse, will heighten your awareness of a character's mood and personal development. For instance, in *Antony and Cleopatra*, the famous military leader Marcus Antony usually speaks in blank verse, but also speaks in fits of prose (II, iii, ll. 43-46) once his masculinity and authority have been questioned. Similarly, in *Timon of Athens*, after the wealthy Lord Timon abandons the city of Athens to live in a cave, he harangues anyone whom he encounters in prose (IV, iii, l. 331 ff.). In contrast, the reader should wonder why the bestial Caliban in *The Tempest* speaks in blank verse rather than in prose.

Implied Stage Action

When we read a Shakespearean play, we are reading a performance text. Actors interact through dialogue, but at the same time these actors cry, gesticulate, throw tantrums, pick up daggers, and compulsively wash murderous "blood" from their hands. Some of the action that takes place on stage is explicitly stated in stage directions. However, some of the stage activity is couched within the dialogue itself. Attentiveness to these cues is important as one conceives how to visualize the action. When Iago in *Othello* feigns concern for Cassio whom he himself has stabbed, he calls to the surrounding men, "Come, come:/Lend me a light" (V, i, ll. 86-87). It is almost sure that one of the actors involved will bring him a torch or lantern. In the same play, Emilia, Desdemona's maidservant, asks if she should fetch her lady's nightgown and Desdemona replies, "No, unpin me here" (IV, iii, l. 37). In *Macbeth*, after killing Duncan,

Macbeth brings the murder weapon back with him. When he tells his wife that he cannot return to the scene and place the daggers to suggest that the king's guards murdered Duncan, she castigates him: "Infirm of purpose/Give me the daggers. The sleeping and the dead are but as pictures" (II, ii, ll. 50-52). As she exits, it is easy to visualize Lady Macbeth grabbing the daggers from her husband.

For 400 years, readers have found it greatly satisfying to work with all aspects of Shakespeare's language—the implied stage action, word choice, sentence structure, and wordplay—until all aspects come to life. Just as seeing a fine performance of a Shakespearean play is exciting, staging the play in one's own mind's eye, and revisiting lines to enrich the sense of the action, will enhance one's appreciation of Shakespeare's extraordinary literary and dramatic achievements.

Historical Background

The primary source for *Othello* is a short story from *Gli Hecatommithi*, a collection of tales published in 1565 by Geraldi Cinthio. The story from the collection dealing with "The Unfaithfulness of Husbands and Wives," provides an ideal place for an Elizabethan dramatist to look for a plot. Since no translation of this work is known to have appeared before 1753, scholars believe that Shakespeare either read the work in its original Italian, or that he was familiar with a French translation of Cinthio's tales, published in 1585 by Gabriel Chappuys.

In Cinthio's tale, the wife is known as Disdemona, but the other characters are designated by titles only. There are also significant differences in the length of time over which the drama takes place, details of setting, and character's actions.

Commentators have also suggested that Pliny's *Natural History* provided Shakespeare with details to enhance Othello's exotic adventures and his alien origins. It has even been suggested by Geoffrey Bullough that Shakespeare consulted John Pory's translation of Leo Africanus' *A Geographical History of Africa* which distinguishes between Moors of northern and southern Africa and characterizes both groups as candid and unaffected, but prone to jealousy. Shakespeare was also familiar with fifteenth and early sixteenth century accounts of wars between Venice and Turkey during which time Venice regained temporary control of Cyprus.

It is agreed by most scholars that Shakespeare wrote Othello in 1604, but some have suggested a composition date as early as 1603 or even 1602. The earliest recorded performance of the play was that by the King's Men "in the Banketinge house at Whit Hall" on November 1, 1604. However, it is also possible that the play was performed earlier that year in a public theater.

Othello was first printed in Quarto form in 1622, and then in the First Folio of 1623; however, there are many variations between the texts of Q1 and F1. The First Folio contains approximately 160 lines that are not in the First Quarto, but it has notably fewer stage directions. In contrast, the First Quarto contains about 13 lines or partial lines not found in the First Folio. Despite the differences, textual commentators generally agree that the Folio edition was printed from a copy of the First Quarto, together with corrections and additions from some reliable manuscript, such as an acting company prompt-book.

During the seventeenth and eighteenth centuries Shakespearean tragedy was revived with leading actors such as Thomas Betterton and Barton Booth playing the role of Othello. Betterton was noted for the "moving and graceful energy with which Othello had addressed the Senate." When Booth "wept, his tears broke from him perforce. He never whimpered, whined or blubbered; in his rage he never mouthed or ranted."

In the nineteenth century, Edmund Kean was described by Samuel Taylor Coleridge as having brought "flashes of lightning" to the interpretation of Shakespeare. Ira Aldridge, the most famous figure in black theater history, played Othello with Edmund Kean as his Iago. However natural a black Othello seems, at that time, it was a novelty to audiences for whom the tradition of a Berber chieftain went virtually unchallenged. Aldridge's performance made a deep impression in America and abroad.

The twentieth century includes notable performances by Paul Robeson whose "tenderness, simplicity, and trust were deeply moving." In 1964 Lawrence Olivier "took London by storm" with his portrayal of Othello. John Gielgud's portrayal of "the disintegration of [Othello's] character was traced with immense power and excellent variety." Iago's role as played by Christopher Plummer and Ian McKellen has been acclaimed.

Cinematic versions of *Othello* are impressive, as is Orson Welles' 1952 interpretation, which has been described as "one of the screen's sublime achievements" by Vincent Canby of the *New York Times*. The most recent interpretation of *Othello* is a film which includes Laurence Fishburne as Othello and Kenneth Branagh as Iago.

Master List of Characters

Roderigo—*A Venetian gentleman; rejected suitor to Desdemona*

Iago—*Newly appointed ensign to Othello, Moor of Venice*

Brabantio—*Venetian Senator; father to Desdemona*

Othello—*The Moorish General; husband to Desdemona*

Cassio—*Newly appointed lieutenant to Othello*

Duke of Venice—*Official who appoints Othello in charge of Cyprian mission*

Desdemona—*Wife to Othello; daughter to Brabantio*

Montano—*Retiring governor of Cyprus; predecessor to Othello in Cyprian government*

Emilia—*Wife to Iago; attendant to Desdemona*

Clown—*Servant to Othello*

Bianca—*A courtesan; mistress to Cassio*

Gratiano—*Venetian nobleman; brother to Brabantio*

Lodovico—*Venetian nobleman; kinsman to Brabantio*

Senators—*Officials who discuss Cyprian mission*

Messengers—*Deliver announcements during the play*

Two Gentlemen—*Converse with the governor*

Third Gentleman—*Bring news of the Turkish fleet*

Herald—*Othello's herald who reads a proclamation*

Sailor—*Brings message about Turkish fleet*

Officers—*Unnamed characters throughout the play who serve in the military.*

Attendants—*Unnamed characters throughout the play whose purpose is to serve the other characters.*

Summary of the Play

On a quiet night in Venice, Iago, ensign to the Moorish general, Othello, enlists the aid of Roderigo in his plot against Othello. Iago secretly hates Othello and tells Roderigo, a rejected suitor to Desdemona, that she has eloped with the Moor. After this revelation, Roderigo and Iago awaken Brabantio, Desdemona's father, with news that she has been transported into Othello's hands. Iago informs Othello of Brabantio's anger. Brabantio arrives with officers to confront Othello, but they are interrupted by Michael Cassio who summons Othello to the Duke of Venice's palace.

The duke and senators welcome Othello and inform him of his deployment to Cyprus in a defensive against the Ottomites. Brabantio accuses Othello of winning Desdemona's affection by magic, after which Othello explains that he won Desdemona's love by sincere means. Desdemona professes her duty to her husband. Subsequently, Othello is sent to Cyprus leaving Iago in charge of Desdemona's safe passage to Cyprus along with Emilia, Iago's wife and Desdemona's attendant. Iago suggests that Roderigo follow Desdemona to Cyprus. Once alone, Iago reveals his plan to implicate Michael Cassio in a clandestine affair with Desdemona.

During a raging storm which destroys the Turkish fleet, Othello and his men land at the Cyprian seaport. By telling Roderigo a lie that Desdemona loves Cassio, Iago now urges Roderigo to incite Cassio to violence. Later that evening at Othello's wedding feast, Iago gets Cassio drunk; as a result, Othello dismisses Cassio from service because of behavior unbecoming a lieutenant. Iago then encourages Cassio to appeal to Desdemona to influence Othello to reinstate Cassio.

Desdemona tells Cassio that she will help him. Cassio leaves quickly, and when Othello arrives, Desdemona pleads for Cassio. Iago uses Cassio's quick exit and Desdemona's pleas to cast doubt on her fidelity and Cassio's integrity.

Desdemona and Emilia enter, and Othello admits to a headache. When Desdemona tries to assuage his illness with her handkerchief, he knocks it down. Emilia picks it up and gives it to Iago. When Othello demands visible proof of Desdemona's infidelity, Iago asserts that he has seen Cassio with the handkerchief. Having become sufficiently suspicious, Othello vows revenge. Later, Cassio gives the handkerchief which Iago hid in Cassio's room to Bianca, his jealous mistress, in order for her to copy.

Riled by Iago's lies and innuendos, Othello succumbs to a trance. After he revives, Iago incites him anew by talking to Cassio about Bianca while Othello eavesdrops on the conversation. Mistakenly, Othello thinks Cassio is boasting about having seduced Desdemona. Bianca enters and throws the handkerchief at Cassio; consequently, Othello, convinced of Desdemona's guilt, swears to kill her.

Lodovico, Brabantio's kinsman, arrives with orders from the duke for Othello to return to Venice, leaving Cassio in charge in Cyprus for which Desdemona expresses pleasure. Othello strikes her, and his actions give Iago cause to suggest that Othello is going mad. Iago then convinces Roderigo that killing Cassio will ensure his chances with Desdemona. Later in the evening, Othello orders Desdemona to wait for him alone in their bed chamber. As she prepares to retire, she sings a song about forsaken love.

At Iago's instigation, Roderigo attacks Cassio who in turn wounds Roderigo. Iago then stabs Cassio so that Othello thinks Iago has kept a promise to kill Cassio. When Roderigo cries out, Iago kills him.

In the bed chamber, while Othello ponders Desdemona's beauty and innocence, she awakens, and Othello commands her to pray before she dies. In spite of her supplications, he suffocates her with a pillow. Emilia enters, and Othello justifies his revenge by claiming the handkerchief as proof of her infidelity. Appalled at this act, Emilia reveals Iago's guilt. Iago enters, kills Emilia, and is arrested. Othello tries to kill Iago, and despite demands for an explanation, Iago remains silent and is led off. Before Othello is led off, he draws a concealed weapon, stabs himself, and kisses Desdemona as he dies.

Estimated Reading Time

An average student should plan to spend at least one hour to read each act of the play for the first reading if the text used provides sufficient footnotes. Subsequent readings will take less time as familiarity with the vocabulary, the story line, and the writer's style increases. *Othello* comprises five acts with a total of 15 scenes, consequently the student might feel comfortable reading three to five scenes at each session, which would entail a total reading time of three to five hours.

Act I

Act I, Scene 1

New Characters:

Iago: *newly appointed ensign to Othello, Moor of Venice*

Roderigo: *gentleman, disappointed suitor to Desdemona*

Brabantio: *Venetian Senator, father to Desdemona*

Summary

One night on a street in Venice, Iago discloses to Roderigo the nature of his hatred for Othello, the Moor of Venice. It seems that in spite of the petitions of three influential Venetians, Othello has by-passed Iago for promotion to lieutenant. Instead, he has chosen Michael Cassio, a Florentine, and has appointed Iago to the less important position of ensign. Iago then enlists the aid of Roderigo, a disappointed suitor to Desdemona, in waking Brabantio, Desdemona's father, with the disturbing news that his household has been robbed. Roderigo then proceeds to inform Brabantio that Desdemona has eloped with Othello. Brabantio recognizes Roderigo as the suitor he forbade to come to his home. Iago interjects Roderigo's information with images of animal lust and leaves telling Roderigo it would not be politic for him to stay, since he is officially Othello's inferior in rank.

Analysis

When Roderigo responds to Iago by saying, "Thou told'st me thou didst hold him in thy hate," it is clear that Iago has previously mentioned his hatred for Othello. Consequently, Iago weaves an intricate plot to undo the Moor. What drives Iago throughout the play is a manipulative duplicity which is inherent in his nature. Samuel Taylor Coleridge called this aspect a "motiveless malignancy," since as the play progresses, Iago seems to be motivated by his pure evil rather than by any external factor or reason he may give for his actions.

The first pawn he enlists in his plan is Roderigo, who had been previously denied courtship of Desdemona by Brabantio. Playing on Roderigo's frustration, Iago gains his trust by telling him that he hates the Moor because Othello preferred to promote Michael Cassio as his honorable lieutenant.

We learn that in spite of the "personal suit" of three influential Venetians who interceded on Iago's behalf, Othello chose "a great arithmetician / One Michael Cassio" as his lieutenant. The biting tone Iago uses to describe Cassio reflects the contempt he feels for him. Moreover, Iago feels that Othello, "loving his own pride and purposes," chose to ignore the petitions of the noblemen and made his choice with "a bombast circumstance." The implication here is that Othello did not make his decision on appropriate grounds. Consequently, throughout his speech to Roderigo, Iago reveals not only his hatred for Othello, but also for Cassio. Iago feels that he has been denied promotion to lieutenant by a man "that never did set a squadron in the field, / Nor division of a battle knows." In addition, he ignores the fact that Othello chose Cassio precisely for this expertise as a tactical soldier and theorist. Iago's contempt for Cassio is evident in the way he demeans Cassio's abilities without recognizing that Othello's choice for lieutenant did not necessarily depend on field experience. Iago offers his own experience in battle "At Rhodes, at Cyprus, and on other grounds" as concrete evidence that he should have been chosen lieutenant. This same jealousy and hatred for Cassio lends credibility to Iago's desire to include Cassio in the plan of destruction that emerges in the play.

Iago's speech also reveals his contention that "preferment goes by letter and affection" rather than by ability. Using himself as an

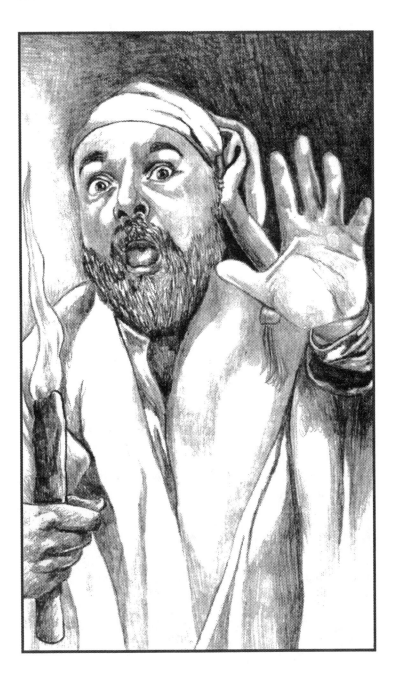

example of how the system works, Iago professes his belief about duty and service. He believes that "we cannot all be masters, nor all masters / Cannot be truly followed," suggesting that Othello is not a master to be followed. In doing so, he begins to justify to himself all that he eventually does to undo the Moor. Iago reveals his contempt for what he sees as "many a duteous and knee-crooking knave" who spends his military career in service to an officer. Then, he indicates his admiration for others "who, trimmed in forms and visages of duty, / Keep yet their hearts attending on themselves." Iago's contempt for the dutiful officer and his respect for the hypocrite reveal his own distorted views of duty and service in the military. He categorizes himself among the hypocrites and indicates that he will serve himself best by serving Othello.

Thus, it is no surprise when he says, "I am not what I am," to Roderigo as an assertion that his "outward action doth demonstrate / The native act and figure" of his heart "In compliment extern" in order to achieve his "peculiar end." This revelation establishes one of the recurring motifs in the play as Iago begins to present different faces to each character in order to win trust, gain confidence, and at the same time remain beyond reproach. When Iago and Roderigo awaken Brabantio and inform him of Desdemona's elopement, much of the contrasting imagery of black and white, lust and love, and illusion and reality is established.

Iago's first remark to Brabantio regarding Desdemona's whereabouts begins a series of images intended to shock Brabantio and rouse hatred for Othello. Iago tells Brabantio that "Even now, now, very now, an old black ram / Is tupping your white ewe." The repetition of the word *now* stresses the immediacy of the action which Iago intends in order to create chaos and confusion. The animal imagery Iago evokes serves several purposes. First, it reveals Iago's perception of love as an animal sexual act, a picture hardly appropriate to present to a father with respect to his daughter. Next, it degrades the love between Othello and Desdemona. Finally, it demonstrates that Iago will intentionally disregard another's feelings to suit his purpose. In the three words *old, black,* and *ram,* Iago stresses Othello's age, emphasizes his color, and strips him of his humanity in Brabantio's presence.

To make the image more potent, Iago tells Brabantio that if

something is not done immediately, "the devil will make a grandsire of you." By comparing Othello to the devil, Iago suggests to Brabantio that Othello possesses a diabolical nature. As the conversation proceeds, it is clear that Brabantio, still not fully awake, has not felt the full impact of Iago's words. Consequently, Iago plays on Brabantio's confusion by stressing that if Brabantio does not act, he will have his "daughter covered with a Barbary horse." Again Iago reduces love to an animal act devoid of its human component. With one final metaphor, Iago tells Brabantio that Desdemona and "the Moor are now making the beast with two backs" in order to incite him against Othello. In this reference, Iago chooses to avoid Othello's name and, instead, refers to his ethnicity.

The success of Iago's attempt to demean Othello is evident when Brabantio says, "This accident is not unlike my dream: / Belief of it oppresses me already," and he calls for a search party. At this point Brabantio is so distraught that he questions whether what he has just learned is a dream or a reality.

Act I, Scene 2

New Characters:

Othello: *Moor of Venice, husband to Desdemona*

Cassio: *Othello's newly appointed lieutenant*

Attendants: *unnamed characters whose purpose is to serve the other characters*

Officers: *unnamed characters who serve in the military*

Summary

Before the Sagittary in Venice, Iago prepares Othello for Brabantio's anger at the elopement of Desdemona and tells Othello that he resisted attacking Brabantio who spoke ill of him. Othello says that his reputation will speak for itself and asserts his sincere love for Desdemona. Michael Cassio then enters summoning Othello to the Duke of Venice for an urgent conference regarding a military expedition to Cyprus. Brabantio, Roderigo, and officers enter ready to attack Othello, but Othello makes it clear that there

is no need to fight. Brabantio demands to know where Desdemona is and accuses Othello of winning her affection through the use of magic. Othello informs Brabantio that he has been summoned by the Duke; an officer concurs; and they all proceed to the conference.

Analysis

The opening of this scene echoes the statement "I am not what I am" with which Iago previously revealed himself to Roderigo. As he speaks to Othello about Brabantio's anger at the elopement of Desdemona, he cleverly plays on Othello's trust in him. Accordingly he tells the Moor that because of Brabantio's "scurvy and provoking terms" he could hardly keep himself from attacking Brabantio in defense of Othello. He presents himself to Othello in a favorable light which emphasizes the hypocrisy and duplicity of his nature. Othello asserts his love for Desdemona with the innocence and purity which Iago also intends to destroy. Subsequently Michael Cassio's announcement that the duke requires the immediate service of Othello is a reminder of Othello's untarnished reputation as a military man in service to the duke. In contrast, Brabantio's abrupt entrance and attempt to discredit Othello's sincerity by accusing him of winning Desdemona "with foul charms" and "with drugs or minerals" suggests a racial aspect to his accusation.

Brabantio's first reference to Othello as a "foul thief" reflects the influence Iago has had on Brabantio. In the previous scene, Roderigo and Iago awakened Brabantio with the declaration that his household had been robbed. This statement planted the image of Othello as a thief in Brabantio's mind. Consequently, when Brabantio confronts Othello, "foul thief" seems to be an appropriate accusation. Brabantio cannot accept the fact that Desdemona would have gone with Othello of her own volition "if she in chains of magic were not bound." It is as if this sort of supernatural or drug-induced seduction is the only one that would make sense— Brabantio is incredulous that Desdemona would have "shunn'd / The wealthy curled darlings of our nation" to "Run from her guardage to the sooty bosom / Of such a thing as Othello." Brabantio's reference to Othello as "such a thing" reduces him to a nonhuman entity, and the image of his "sooty bosom" recalls Iago's emphasis on Othello's skin color. There is a definite sense that the fact that Othello is an African makes this whole situation harder for Brabantio to accept, which is significant toward our understanding of Othello at this stage. Roderigo has already referred to Othello as "the thick-lips." Later, Iago calls him "the black Othello," pointing out the external features that separate Othello from the Venetian community.

Act I, Scene 3

New Characters:

Duke of Venice: *official who appoints Othello to Cyprus*

Senators: *officials who discuss Cyprian mission*

Sailor: *brings in a message about the Turkish fleet*

Messenger: *delivers messages to various characters throughout the play*

Desdemona: *daughter to Brabantio; wife to Othello*

Summary

In a Senate chamber, the Duke of Venice and senators discuss the number of galleys comprising a Turkish fleet headed for Cyprus. A sailor enters with a message that the Turkish fleet is preparing for Rhodes, which the duke and senators agree may be a diversionary tactic. When a messenger enters with news from Montano, the Governor of Cyprus, that the Ottomites have joined the fleet at Rhodes, the duke and senators are convinced that Cyprus is in danger of attack. Brabantio, Othello, Cassio, Iago, and Roderigo enter, and Brabantio tells the duke that Desdemona has been tricked by Othello who tells the duke that he did indeed win Desdemona's affections, but not by any drugs or medicine. He tells how, as a guest in Brabantio's house, his tales of dangerous adventure intrigued Desdemona and how her pity for his pains turned to love for him. Desdemona enters and respectfully establishes her dilemma as a "divided duty" between her father and Othello and asserts that her preference for her husband is natural "so much

duty as my mother show'd / To you, preferring you before her father." The matter is settled, and the duke assigns Othello to Cyprus.
Desdemona suggests she go with him, and Othello leaves Iago in
charge of Desdemona's transport to Cyprus along with Emilia, Iago's
wife, as her attendant. Roderigo reasserts his love for Desdemona,
and once he and Iago are alone, Iago convinces him that she will
soon tire of the Moor and turn to Roderigo. Alone, Iago thinks of a
ruse to suggest Desdemona's infidelity with Cassio.

Analysis

The action of the play moves forward as the duke and the senators discuss the discrepancy of some reports from the Cyprian front.
This event establishes the urgency for Othello's assignment to
Cyprus as his military duty interrupts his newly acquired duty as a
husband to Desdemona. The timing of the event also takes the
action to an exotic locale and places Othello in "most disastrous
chances" not only in military terms but also in terms of Iago's
treacherous plot to destroy Othello and all that he represents.
Othello's implicit trust in Iago leaves him vulnerable to Iago's malevolent nature, and in order for Iago's plotting to be credible, his
attempts at gaining everyone's trust must be successful.

Brabantio's claim to the duke that Othello used "spells and
medicines bought of mountebanks" to entrap Desdemona is con-
tradicted by Othello's "round unvarnished tale" of how he sincerely
won Desdemona's love and affection. Desdemona's subsequent
assertion that she "profess / Due to the Moor" clearly establishes
that Othello is what he appears to be. Brabantio's accusation that
Othello is "an abuser of the world, a practicer / Of arts inhibited
and out of warrant" along with Iago's previous attempts to demean
Othello to Roderigo contain the racial charge that Othello must
have used some kind of magic or sorcery to seduce Desdemona.
His accusation assumes that this is the only reason she would by-
pass "the wealthy curled darlings" of Venice for a man of a different race.

Othello's speech to the Senate reveals the honest, unaffected
manner with which he presents himself as he opens his address
with "Most potent, brave, and reverend signiors / My very noble,
and approved good masters." Othello answers Brabantio's charge

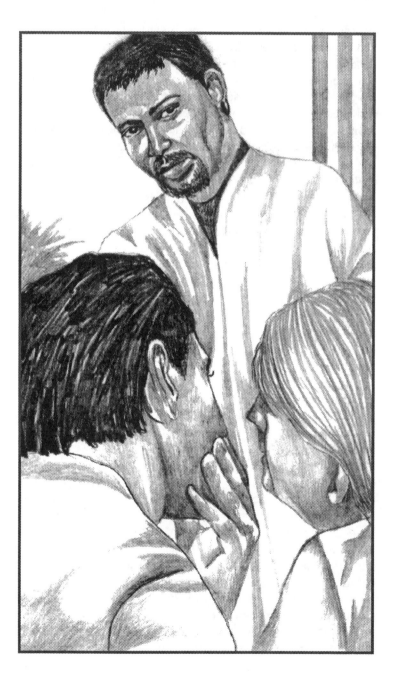

by acknowledging his marriage to Desdemona not by denying it. His tone is sincere and not defensive, and he demonstrates humility without ingratiating himself before the esteemed council. Othello is aware of his unsophisticated speech and manner when he says "Rude am I in my speech, / And little blessed with the soft phrase of peace." However, he maintains his dignity while speaking with the impressive Venetian council as he "will a round unvarnished tale deliver" about how he won Desdemona. At this point Brabantio is quick to interject his belief that Desdemona must have been tricked by some magic because "in spite of nature / Of years, of country, credit, everything" she defied all logic and fell in love with Othello. Othello continues his speech with his story of battles, seiges, fortunes" through "rough quarries, rocks, and hills," and the pattern in his speech reflects a rhythm that echoes the adventurous spirit with which Desdemona fell in love.

According to Othello, when he told his adventurous tales "of the Cannibals that each other eat, / The Anthropophagi, and men whose heads / Do grow beneath their shoulders," Desdemona became enthralled and "with a greedy ear" would "devour up [his] discourse." After hearing a few tales, Desdemona wanted to know more, so Othello took the time to tell her. At such stories, Desdemona would express sympathy and compassion for his hardships and in the end felt "'twas strange, 'twas passing strange; / 'Twas pitiful, 'twas wondrous pitiful." Her reaction suggests the awe she felt and the admiration she showed for his dangerous deeds. Othello concludes that Desdemona "loved [him] for the dangers [he] had passed," and he in turn "loved her that she did pity him." Such is his "witchcraft." Even the duke comments to Brabantio, "I think this tale would win my daughter too," attesting to the veracity of Othello's story.

When Desdemona is called upon to explain where she "owes obedience," she replies with respect toward her father and confidence in what she believes. In a convincing statement, Desdemona admits obedience to her father "for life and education" but as a wife she must "profess / Due to the Moor." It is clear that Desdemona made her decision to marry Othello in a rational state of mind rather than in the drug-induced state of mind for which Othello has been held responsible. Her "divided duty" does not

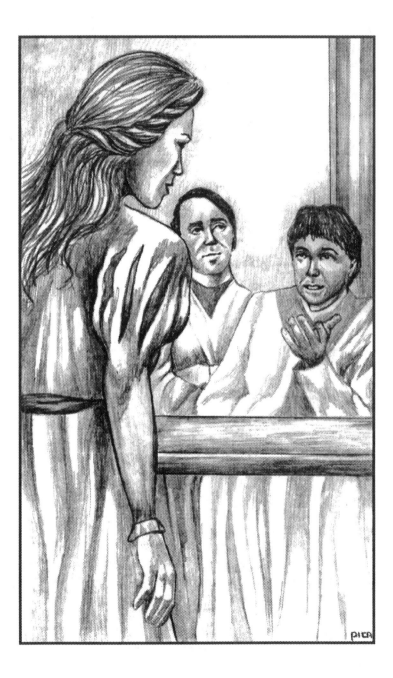

negate her responsibility as a daughter, but only adds another responsibility as a wife. Desdemona reminds her father that this same preference was made once by her mother. Desdemona's pronouncement supports Othello's story, and Brabantio has no choice but to drop the issue of Othello's witchcraft.

When Othello entrusts Desdemona to Iago for safe passage to Cyprus, he unwittingly places himself in a position to become a pawn in Iago's web of deceit as evinced by Iago's comment that "the Moor is of a free and open nature / That thinks men honest that but seem to be so, / And will as tenderly be led by the nose / As asses are."

At the end of Scene 3, Iago expresses his attitude toward love when Roderigo hints at drowning himself because he cannot live without Desdemona. Roderigo says he is ashamed of being so in love, yet "it is not in [his] virtue to amend it." Iago's immediate reaction to Roderigo's lack of will indicates the attitude that what we are determined by our own will. At this point, it is clear that Iago himself determines the evil he perpetrates. There are no extenuating circumstances. For Iago, a man's reason controls the baser instincts of which love is "merely a lust of the blood and a permission of the will." Iago cannot comprehend love in terms of its virtue because he cannot rise above the level of his own baseness. From his vantage point, he debases all the goodness he sees around him. Consequently, Othello and Desdemona's love to him is "a violent commencement" which will result in "an answerable sequestration." Iago suggests that Othello will tire of Desdemona and "the food that to him now is as luscious as locusts" will become "shortly as bitter as coloquintida." Likewise, when Desdemona "is sated with his body," she will turn to someone else. The specific imagery of food and appetite with respect to love is significant because it points out that Iago reduces love to merely a sexual appetite void of emotion.

To give further insight into his nature, Iago states a reason for his hatred of Othello in a brief soliloquy. He says, "it is thought abroad that 'twixt my sheets / He has done my service" implying that Othello committed adultery with Emilia. Rumor is as sufficient as truth to breed hatred in Iago. Perhaps his own growing jealousy motivates him to create jealousy in Othello.

As Iago takes into account all that he has observed, he realizes that his best access to Othello lies in Othello's trust. Iago feels no compuction about betraying that trust as a means to an end. This behavior is consistent with what we have seen of him thusfar.

Study Questions

1. What reason does Iago give for his hatred of Othello?

2. What information do Roderigo and Iago give to Brabantio regarding Desdemona's whereabouts?

3. How does Iago make himself look favorable in Othello's eyes?

4. What news does Michael Cassio bring when he enters?

5. To what does Brabantio attribute Desdemona's affections for Othello?

6. What is the military issue that the Duke of Venice and his senators discuss?

7. What accusation does Brabantio make against Othello to the duke?

8. What explanation does Othello give as cause for Desdemona's affection for him?

9. To whom does Desdemona pledge her duty?

10. In the final speech of Act I, what does Iago plan to do to further his plot against Othello?

Answers

1. Iago tells Roderigo that he hates Othello because "Michael Cassio, a Florentine / ...that never set a squadron in the field / Nor the division of a battle knows," has just been chosen by Othello as his lieutenant. His bitterness is evident when he tells Roderigo that "'tis the curse of service" that promotion is made by personal liking not by seniority.

2. After Roderigo calls out in the night that thieves have robbed Brabantio's household, Iago tells Brabantio, in gross images of animal lust, that "an old black ram / Is tupping your white ewe." When he refers to Othello as the devil, he incites

Brabantio further against the Moor. Roderigo then informs Brabantio that Desdemona has been "Transported... / To the gross clasps of a lascivious Moor."

3. Iago makes himself look favorable in Othello's eyes by telling him how Brabantio's "scurvy and provoking terms" against Othello made him want to attack Brabantio. He also suggests that Othello watch his marriage because Brabantio might invoke the law against it, thus playing on Othello's trust in him.

4. Michael Cassio tells Othello that the duke requires his service because of some military action, "a business of some kind," in Cyprus.

5. Brabantio attributes Desdemona's affection for Othello to his having "enchanted her" because this attraction is so opposite her nature and breeding. He emphasizes Othello's exotic nature in order to minimize the plausibility that Desdemona could choose someone who is not amount "the wealthy curled darlings of our nation."

6. The duke and the senators are in the process of determining the validity of reports that say "a hundred and seven," "a hundred forty," and "two hundred" Turkish galleys are approaching Cyprus. A sailor enters with a false report from Signor Angelo that the Turks are making for Rhodes, but a messenger from Signor Montano, governor of Cyprus, reports that the Ottomites have joined the Turkish fleet and are bearing toward Cyprus.

7. When Brabantio arrives at the duke's he says that Desdemona has been "abused...stolen...and corrupted / By spells and medicines bought of mountebanks" in order to accuse Othello of entrapping his daughter.

8. Othello explains that he has taken Desdemona away, but not in the way Brabantio accuses him. His "round unvarnished tale" explains how, as a guest in Brabantio's house, he told his adventures of danger and world experiences. At such times, Desdemona would hear his stories "but still the house affairs would draw her thence" and then she would return

to hear more. When he filled in the details of his stories, Desdemona "swore, in faith, 'twas strange, 'twas passing strange; / 'Twas pitiful, 'twas wondrous pitiful," and loved him for the dangers he experienced.

9. Desdemona perceives "a divided duty" between her father and her husband, and as her mother had shown allegiance to her husband, so Desdemona professes "Due to the Moor."

10. After Iago has successfully entrapped Roderigo, he convinces Roderigo not to drown himself and fills Roderigo with anticipation that Desdemona may tire of the Moor and turn to him. Iago then sees a way to "plume up" his "will in double knavery" by suggesting to Othello that Michael Cassio is secretly enamored of Desdemona and that they are on a too familiar basis with each other.

Suggested Essay Topics

1. Explain how Iago uses his power of persuasion with Roderigo, Brabantio, and Othello to create his scheme to undo the Moor.

2. Contrast what Iago says about Othello with what Othello reveals about himself through his own words.

Act II

Act II, Scene 1

New Characters:

Montano: *Governor of Cyprus*

Two Gentlemen: *converse with the governor*

A third Gentlemen: *brings news of the Turkish fleet*

Emilia: *wife to Iago; attendant to Desdemona*

Summary

At a seaport in Cyprus, near the harbor, Montano and two gentlemen discuss the storm raging off the coast. A third gentleman enters with news that the storm has destroyed the Turkish fleet and that Michael Cassio has arrived. Cassio enters expressing hopes for Othello's safe arrival in Cyprus. A messenger arrives with the news of the arrival of another ship, and Cassio directs the second gentleman to find out whose it is. The second gentleman re-enters announcing the arrival of Iago's ship. Desdemona enters, asking Cassio for news of Othello, and he assures her that Othello is well. Desdemona and Emilia engage in some banter with Iago, and after the word play, Iago carefully notices how Michael Cassio courteously greets Desdemona.

Othello then enters content that the war is over and jubilant at seeing Desdemona safe. Subsequently, he directs everyone to the castle and tells Iago to disembark the spoils of war. Alone with

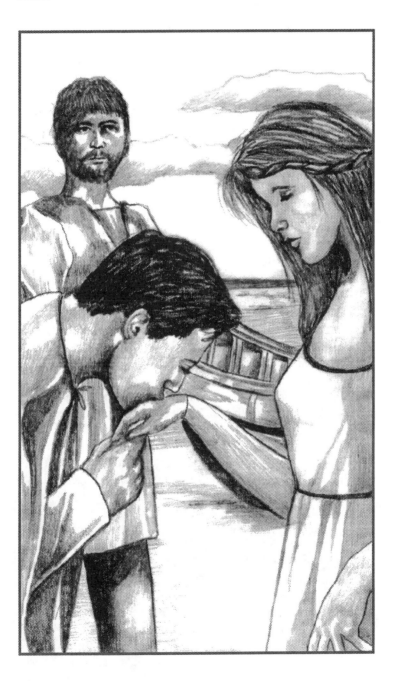

Roderigo, Iago tells him that Desdemona is in love with Cassio and that when her appetite for the Moor wanes, Cassio is the one to whom she will turn. Roderigo expresses disbelief at this observation, so Iago describes the warm greeting Cassio gave Desdemona. Next, he urges Roderigo to instigate Cassio to anger and provoke him to a fight. He convinces Roderigo that once Cassio is removed, he will have a better chance with Desdemona. Alone, Iago expresses his suspicion of Emilia's infidelity with Othello, his desire for revenge, and his plan to have Othello trust him more.

Analysis

The opening scene of this act serves several dramatic functions. First, Montano's discussion with the two gentlemen provides a panoramic view of the intensity of the storm with "a high-wrought flood," "the wind-shaked surge, with high and monstrous mane," and "the enchafed flood." The imagery used to describe the sea suggests the fury of a wild beast with which it rages. Consequently, portraying a storm of this magnitude would present a difficulty on the Elizabethan stage. This description also makes plausible the news that the storm has destroyed the Turkish fleet. In addition, the scene justifies Cassio's concern for Othello when he says, "O let the heavens / Give him defense against the elements / For I have lost him on a dangerous sea!" The irony here is that Othello's enemy is not the war nor the sea but Iago who has safely landed in Cyprus. Cassio's comment that "Tempests themselves...the guttered rocks...congregated sands, / Traitors...as having a sense of beauty, do omit / Their mortal natures" personifies a treacherous sea with a benevolent nature in sparing Desdemona. This image contrasts the malevolent nature of Iago who is a traitor sparing no one to undo Othello.

To offset the intensity of the opening of the act, Desdemona and Emilia engage in some light humor with Iago prompted by Cassio's greeting of Emilia. After Cassio kisses Emilia, Iago remarks, "Sir, would she give you so much of her lips / As of her tongue she oft bestows on me, / You would have enough." This quip begins a series of "praises" of women by Iago under the guise of light banter with serious overtones that suit Iago's duplicity as one who says one thing yet means another, even in humor. After the ironic word play, Iago carefully notices how Cassio greets Desdemona when he "takes her by the palm …smile[s] upon her …kissed [his] three fingers so oft" in a gallant gesture. Iago takes this innocent gesture and gives it an evil motive later to convince Roderigo of their secret love. Iago's comment that "with as little a web as this I will ensnare as great a fly as Cassio" suggests the image of a spider weaving a web to trap it victim. Like the spider, Iago is weaving a web of deceit to capture the unsuspecting Cassio.

Othello enters and expresses his joy at seeing Desdemona; Desdemona reciprocates the feeling. In an aside Iago remarks, "you are well tuned now! / But I'll set down pegs that make this music / Honest as I am." The music imagery suggested by his comment is that Desdemona and Othello are instruments to be played upon and manipulated. Again Iago takes something pure and debases it.

In the last part of the scene, Iago uses Cassio's courtly greeting of Desdemona as proof of their love. When Roderigo expresses disbelief, Iago says that when the same appetite with which she loved Othello "is made dull with the act of sport" she will turn to Cassio. Again, Iago expresses his view that Desdemona's attraction for Othello is an appetite wherein "her eyes must be fed." When Roderigo still expresses disbelief, Iago adds, "Didst thou not see her paddle with the palm of his hand?" intimating that this innocent greeting is an act of lechery. Having cast sufficient doubt about Desdemona's virtue, Iago instructs Roderigo to "find some occasion to anger Cassio…provoke him that he may" strike Roderigo to insure the displanting of Cassio.

In his soliloquy, Iago reveals the motivation which compels him to plan and execute his devious plot. Once again, Iago takes inventory of what he has observed as he did at the end of Act I, Scene 3. He believes Cassio loves Desdemona and that Desdemona loves Cassio. This is true. However, their love is not adulterous; it is a genuine cordiality for one another. Eventually, Iago will cast dubious motives on this mutual affection in order to suit his own needs. Iago also believes that Othello is "of a constant, loving, noble nature." This is also true, and it becomes the means through which Iago gains access to Othello's vulnerability. Iago even goes as far as to say he loves Desdemona "not out of absolute lust," but merely as a means to feed his own plan of revenge. As his scheme begins to take shape, his suspicions about Emilia's fidelity "gnaw [his] inwards." This glimpse into Iago's feelings provide the reason for his insatiable appetite for revenge which "nothing can or shall content" until he is "evened with him." The details of Iago's scheme begin to materialize, yet they are not completely solid. If he can't prove Desdemona false, he hopes at least to incite Othello's jealousy to the point at which reason will not abate it. He will get Cassio at a disadvantage and demean him to Othello in such a way that Othello will trust Iago more. Iago adds parenthetically that he even suspects Cassio's adultery with Emilia. Perhaps the jealousy that Iago hopes to instill in Othello is a projection of his own unbridled jealousy for which he has no solid basis. Iago says that his plan "tis here, but yet confused. / Knavery's plain face is never seen till used." He personifies his scheme as if it were a partner of his whose face is indistinct until such time as they meet with mutual purpose.

Act II, Scene 2

New Character:

Herald: *Othello's herald who reads a proclamation*

Summary

In this brief scene before Othello's castle, a Herald enters reading a proclamation of Othello's plans for a feast to honor the defeat of the Turkish fleet and to celebrate his marriage to Desdemona.

Analysis

The dramatic purpose of this scene is, of course, to establish the celebration for the victory over the Turkish fleet and Othello's marriage to Desdemona. However, it also serves as an ironic backdrop for Iago's treachery which is going to be acted out on the streets of Cyprus as Iago sets his trap to discredit Cassio to Montano and Othello.

Act II, Scene 3

Summary

Othello and Desdemona enter the castle along with Cassio and attendants. Othello directs Cassio to stand guard and not to overdo the celebrating, and Cassio replies that he will personally see to it. Othello then informs Cassio that he will speak to him tomorrow and exits with Desdemona. Iago then enters, and Cassio informs him that they should stand watch to which Iago replies that Othello has dismissed them early. Next, he urges Cassio to have a drink to Othello with the other young men who are celebrating, but Cassio informs him that he has already drunk enough. However, at Iago's insistence, Cassio goes off to get the others. Alone Iago says that if Cassio is drunk, he will be easily provoked to argument with Roderigo and the three other men who have been drinking.

Cassio, Montano, and a gentleman enter, and Iago engages Cassio in some toasting and singing. When Cassio exits, Iago tells Montano that Cassio's weakness is drinking to which Montano replies that Othello should be informed. Cassio, drunk, enters chasing Roderigo who has provoked a fight at Iago's prompt. In an attempt to stop Cassio's attack on Roderigo, Montano takes Cassio's arm after which Cassio verbally threatens Montano and fights with him. Othello enters during the scuffle and breaks it up. When he asks what is going on, Iago says that while he and Montano were speaking a fellow came crying for help while being chased by Cassio. Iago adds that Montano tried to stop Cassio while he himself pursued the other who got away. When he returned, he found Montano and Cassio fighting until Othello parted them. Othello dismisses Cassio from service, and all but Cassio and Iago exit. Cassio bemoans his reputation, and Iago tells him that he should go to Desdemona to plead his case. Alone, Iago schemes to suggest to Othello that Desdemona lusts after Cassio.

When Roderigo enters, he is disillusioned and says that he is going back to Venice. However, Iago tells him to be patient, because the plan is in action. Finally, Iago decides to have Emilia intercede with Desdemona for Cassio and to have Othello find Cassio speaking to Desdemona.

Analysis

This scene focuses on Iago's plan to get Cassio involved in a compromising position and sully his reputation. First, he blatantly contradicts Othello's order to Cassio "to look...to the guard tonight" by telling Cassio that Othello "cast us thus early for the love of his Desdemona." After establishing a brief conversation about Desdemona, Iago suggests that Cassio "have a measure to the health of black Othello" to which Cassio replies that he has "very poor and unhappy brains for drinking." However, with some encouragement by Iago, Cassio assents. Iago's treachery is clear when he says, "'mongst this flock of drunkards / Am I to put our Cassio in some action / That may offend the isle."

To further his plan, Iago engages Cassio in rounds of drinking and toasting with Montano and the others. Iago uses this as proof to Montano that Cassio is "a soldier fit to stand by Caesar," but his vice "Tis to his virtue a just equinox" to discredit Cassio's suitability as Othello's lieutenant. Iago's plan culminates in this scene when Cassio re-enters chasing Roderigo threatening to "beat the knave into a twiggen bottle." When Montano intercedes on Roderigo's behalf, Cassio threatens to "knock [him] o'er the mazzard." When Othello enters, stops the fight, and demands an explanation, Iago recounts the incidents and says, "I had rather have this tongue cut from my mouth / Than it should do offense to Michael Cassio." The irony here, as in many of Iago's speeches, is clear. His statement belies all that he has contrived to discredit Cassio. The humiliation of Cassio is complete when Othello says, "Cassio I love thee; / But never more be officer of mine." After his dismissal, Cassio laments the loss of his reputation which gives Iago another opportunity to dishonor Cassio. Iago tells him to seek Desdemona and "importune her help to put you in your place again."

In yet another attempt to disgrace Cassio in Othello's eyes, Iago says that "whiles this honest fool / Plies Desdemona to repair his fortune / ... I'll pour...into [Othello's] ear / That she repeals him for her body's lust." By this time, Iago's plan is becoming more involved as he makes use of coincidence to further his scheme. He is also more determined in his approach as he calls his lies "this pestilence" to be poured into Othello's ear. This comment suggests a scene from Shakespeare's play, *Hamlet*, in which a troop of players

enact "The Murder of Gonzago." In the play-within-a-play, the murderer pours poison into the king's ear while he sleeps in a re-creation of King Hamlet's murder. An Elizabethan audience would not miss the image since the ear was believed to provide access for poisonous substances to enter the body. Iago's poison consists of the lies he plans to tell Othello little by little as if administering drops of poison into his body. Since Othello listens intently to what Iago says, the metaphor is an appropriate one for Iago to create.

As Iago envisions this plan, he relishes the opportunity to turn Desdemona's "virtue into pitch." The contrast of black and white is evident in this image as Iago hopes to defile Desdemona's good-ness. The black/white contrast also emphasizes the color differ-ence between Desdemona and Othello which has been a source of contention with Brabantio's acceptance of Othello and Iago's hatred for him. In this scene, it is clear that Iago manipulates situ-ations to suit his needs, and he takes harmless situations and pre-sents them in an evil light. His soliloquy reveals that once again "knavery's plain face" becomes clear to him as he decides to use Desdemona's own innocence and virtue against her by making "the net / That shall enmesh them all." This image that Iago creates suggests the catch a fisherman might make when he hauls in a net containing a plentiful supply of fish. Like the fisherman, Iago ensnares the unsuspecting characters in his net of trickery and deceit.

Study Questions

1. What dramatic function does the conversation between Montano and the two gentlemen serve?

2. Why does Iago carefully observe the way Cassio greets Desdemona?

3. What information does Iago use to spark Roderigo's interest in his plan to discredit Cassio?

4. What "proof" does Iago use to convince Roderigo that Cassio and Desdemona are lovers?

5. Why does Iago instigate Roderigo to provoke Cassio to a fight?

6. Why does Iago urge Cassio to drink to Othello?

7. What happens when Cassio enters chasing Roderigo?

8. How does Iago plan to bait Othello into doubting Desdemona's fidelity?

9. What does Iago tell Cassio to do to restore the reputation he has sullied in Othello's eyes?

10. How does Iago plan to intensify Othello's doubt about Desdemona?

Answers

1. The conversation between Montano and the two gentlemen serves several functions. It provides a vivid description of the storm as a substitute for staging which would be difficult to accomplish in the Elizabethan theater. It also makes the news of the destruction of the Turkish fleet more credulous. In addition, it provides a reason for Cassio's concern for Othello's safety. Moreover, it points out the irony of Othello's surviving war and the elements only to be destroyed by one whom he trusts most.

2. Iago's careful observation of Cassio's greeting of Desdemona points out how he uses situations to his advantage. He takes this friendly greeting and plans "[w]ith as little a web as this...[to] ensnare as great a fly as Cassio."

3. Iago tells Roderigo that "Desdemona is directly in love with [Cassio]" in order to stir Roderigo's jealousy toward Cassio so that Roderigo will easily comply with a plan to get Cassio out of the way. As a manipulator, Iago uses Roderigo to suit his own purposes with no concern for Roderigo.

4. When Roderigo finds it incredulous that Desdemona and Cassio could be lovers, Iago adds that "they met so near with their lips that their breaths embraced together." Iago's lascivious nature motivates him to give their cordial greeting a lecherous overtone.

5. Iago urges Roderigo to provoke Cassio to a fight so that with

"the impediment most profitably removed" Roderigo will "have a shorter journey to [his] desires." Iago says that he is helping Roderigo, when in fact he is working against him.

6. Iago tells Cassio to drink "to have a measure to the health of black Othello" because "'tis a night of revels." However, Iago's true motive is to get Cassio drunk so "He'll be as full of quarrels and offense" and get involved "in some action / That may offend the isle." Iago says one thing but means another.

7. Cassio threatens to beat Roderigo, and when Montano intercedes on Roderigo's behalf, Cassio verbally threatens to "knock [him] o'er the mazzard." This suits Iago's plan for Montano to witness Cassio in a compromising position.

8. Iago plans to tell Othello that Desdemona pleads for Cassio because of "her body's lust" and that the strength of her plea indicates the intensity of her lust.

9. Iago tells Cassio to go to Desdemona and "entreat her to splinter" the rift between him and Othello. Iago appears to be motivated to help Cassio, but in actuality, he wants to further his own plan to discredit him to Othello.

10. While Cassio is pleading his case to Desdemona, Iago plans to bring Othello at the very moment "when he may Cassio find / Soliciting his wife. In this way he can nurture the seed that he has already planted in Othello's mind concerning Desdemona's infidelity.

Suggested Essay Topics

1. Verbal irony is a dramatic technique by which characters say the opposite of what they mean. Identify examples of verbal irony and explain the difference between what is said and what is meant.

2. In Act II, Iago's scheme to undo Othello becomes more calculated and involves more victims. Explain the steps he takes to achieve his goal and how he traps his victims.

Act III

Act III, Scene 1

New Character:

Clown: *comedic figure from the castle; servant to Othello*

Summary

In this scene before Othello's castle, Cassio enters with two musicians and tells them he will pay them to serenade Othello and Desdemona. A clown enters and comments on the musicians' instruments and tells them that Othello does not want to hear any more music. After the musicians leave, Cassio asks the clown to tell Emilia he wants to see Desdemona. Iago enters and Cassio tells him what he just asked the clown, and Iago tells him he will go get Emilia, and he will keep Othello away. Emilia enters and tells Cassio that Othello and Desdemona are discussing the incident between Cassio and Montano and that she will arrange a meeting.

Analysis

This scene provides some comic relief from the drama that has transpired in the previous act. Cassio's request for the musicians to serenade Othello and Desdemona reflects the Elizabethan custom of awakening people of high rank with serenades on special occasions. When they play, a clown comes out and comments on the quality of their music by asking, "Why, masters, have your instruments been at Naples, that they speak i' th' nose thus?" An

Elizabethan audience would be quick to pick up on the bawdy pun on the word *instruments* and the suggestion of the poor health conditions of the city of Naples. The clown then sarcastically says that Othello likes the music so much, he will pay the musicians to stop. After Iago enters, Cassio tells him he requested to see Desdemona, and Iago says he will "devise a means to draw the Moor / Out of the way" so they can speak more freely. Iago makes it seem as if he is helping Iago's cause; whereas, in reality he is setting up the situation for Othello to find Cassio and Desdemona speaking. When Emilia tells Cassio that Desdemona "speaks for [him] stoutly," Cassio hopes that his conversation with her will then prove fruitful.

Act III, Scene 2

Summary

Within the castle, Othello gives Iago letters to deliver to the senate. Othello and gentlemen walk along the fortress walls.

Analysis

This brief scene presents Othello in a situation where he carries out the duties of the office as a commander.

Act III, Scene 3

Summary

In the garden of the castle, Desdemona tells Cassio that she will do all she can to help him. Emilia adds that Iago is just as distressed by the whole incident. Othello and Iago enter as Cassio leaves, and Iago suggests that there is something suspicious in the way he left. Desdemona asks Othello to call Cassio back, but he says he will speak to him some other time. She insists and pleads Cassio's case, so having enough, Othello says he'll give her what she wants, and asks to be left alone. Iago asks about Cassio's familiarity with Desdemona, and Othello tells him he was in their company many times when they were courting. Othello asks Iago to tell him his thoughts, as vile as they may be, so Iago tells him to

watch out for jealousy. Othello says he'll need more to doubt her, so Iago tells him to observe Desdemona with Cassio and adds that most Venetian women are deceptive using Desdemona's elopement as proof of how she deceived Brabantio. Othello vacillates between doubt and certainty of Desdemona, and Iago leaves him with his thoughts.

Desdemona enters to tell him the dinner guests are waiting, and Othello replies that he has a headache. Desdemona proceeds to wipe his brow with her handkerchief, but when he pushes it away, the handkerchief drops. Emilia picks it up, and when Iago enters she says she has the handkerchief which Iago immediately snatches from her. Othello returns and asks for more tangible proof of her infidelity. Iago mentions that he saw Cassio wipe his beard with the handkerchief. At this, Othello swears vengence and Iago agrees to help him. They discuss the death of Michael Cassio.

Analysis

When Emilia comments that the rift between Othello and Cassio "grieves [her] husband / As if the cause were his" we see how Iago has managed to deceive his own wife who doesn't suspect the evil in his nature. This is an example of dramatic irony in which the character is not aware of vital information as the audience or reader is. Desdemona's further remark, with reference to Iago, "that's an honest fellow," is as ironic because she is not aware of the treachery being connived either. Iago and Othello enter, and Iago says "Ha! I like not that," with reference to Cassio's leaving. When Othello asks him if that was Cassio he saw leaving, Iago replies with feigned uncertainty that he thinks not "that he would steal away so guilty-like" suggesting that there is something inappropriate in Cassio's visit with Desdemona. The conversation that follows between Othello and Iago consists of a series of half thoughts and insinuations by Iago to raise Othello's suspicions about Cassio. As they speak, Othello comments how Iago "didst contract and purse [his] brow together, / As if [he] then [had] shut up in [his] brain / Some horrible conceit." The gestures suggested by Othello's statements are carefully orchestrated by Iago to generate more curiosity and prompt Othello to say "Show me thy thought" which gives Iago the opportunity he wants to plant his

"worst of thoughts / The worst of words" in Othello's mind. Iago responds with the admonition to "beware, my lord, of jealousy! / It is the green-eyed monster, which doth mock / The meat it feeds on." When Othello expresses doubt about there being anything to be jealous of, "For she had eyes and chose me," he says to Iago, "when I doubt, prove." To weaken Othello's confidence, Iago replies, "observe her well with Cassio...I know our country disposition well / In Venice they do let heaven see the pranks / They dare not show their husbands." He seizes upon the opportunity to play upon the fact that Othello is an exotic by suggesting that he is not aware of the deceptive ways of Venetian women. He adds, "She did deceive her father, marrying you," so much so that Brabantio "thought 'twas witchcraft. Iago uses Othello's susceptibility to the belief in magic to feed his doubts. Iago raises the issue of Othello's cultural differences with Desdemona which leads Othello to ponder his color, degree of sophistication, and age as he says that perhaps "For I am black / And have not those soft parts of conversation ...or ...am declined / Into the vale of years."

The conversation has left Othello in a highly charged emotional state, so when Desdemona enters, he tells her he has a headache, and she replies, "let me bind it hard," with her handkerchief, the "first remembrance from the Moor." He pushes the handkerchief away, and it falls to the ground. Emilia picks it up, and Iago immediately snatches it when he enters. This gives him the unexpected "ocular proof" which Othello soon demands in order to be convinced of Desdemona's infidelity.

In a brief soliloquy, Iago recognizes the effect he is having as "the Moor already changes with my poison." Iago continues the metaphor he created in Act II, Scene 3 in which he compared his lies to a pestilence he would pour into Othello's ear. At this point in his scheme, Iago has sufficiently aroused Othello's jealousy so that all the undetectable ministrations of poison "which at the first were scarce found to distaste" have begun to "burn like the mines of sulphur" as they course through Othello's body. Iago is convinced that "not poppy, nor mandragora, / Nor all the drowsy syrups of the world / Shall ever medicine thee to that sweet sleep." Othello has received a lethal dose of Iago's poison, so that all the restoratives in the world cannot counter the fatal effects.

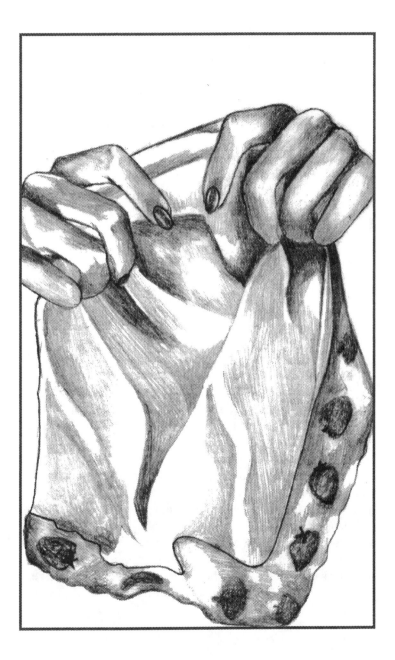

What follows next in the scene is a cleverly manipulated conversation once Iago has caused Othello to have serious doubts about Desdemona's fidelity. When Othello returns, it is clear that he has been plagued by doubts as evident in his remark "Ha! Ha! False to me?" Iago's poison is manifesting itself in Othello's mind, but Iago understates its effect with his emphatic "Why, how now, General. No more of that!" Othello tries to convince himself that what he doesn't see will not harm him, even "if the general camp...had tasted her body." However, at this thought Othello loses touch with reality and fears he is losing his mind, the very source of pride in for his career as a military leader. When his senses return he demands "ocular proof" of Desdemona's infidelity beyond a doubt. Othello warns Iago that if he "dost slander her and torture me" may he be damned for ever.

This scene represents the turning point for Othello as he borders on doubt and certainty with respect to Desdemona's fidelity and Iago's honesty. This is exactly the point of vulnerability Iago needs to ensure that his plan will work. Iago comments that Othello is "eaten up with passion," and he proceeds to conjure images of animal lust to rouse Othello even further. By evoking scenes of Desdemona and Cassio "as prime as goats, as hot as monkeys, / As salt as wolves in pride," Iago heightens Othello's jealousy and desire for proof of her infidelity. Iago abuses Othello's trust by pretending to be painfully honest in that he heard Cassio cry out, "Sweet Desdemona!" in his sleep. Consequently, Othello's rage manifests itself with his threat "to tear her to pieces." Iago hypocritically suggests that "she may be honest yet" and then plants the lie that he saw Cassio wipe his beard with Desdemona's handkerchief. Given the significance of the handkerchief to Othello, it is no surprise that Othello's rage turns to vengeance as he exclaims, "Arise, black vengeance, from the hollow Hell!" Othello, "eaten up with passion," vows revenge and tells Iago he wants to "hear thee say / That Cassio's not alive." This scene progresses from Iago's planting seeds of doubt in Othello's mind to Othello's vowing vengeance with Cassio's death and "some swift means of death for the fair devil."

Act III, Scene 4

New Character:

Bianca: *mistress to Cassio*

Summary

Desdemona asks a clown where Cassio is so that he can be told that Othello is moved considering the incident. She wonders where her handkerchief is, and Emilia says she does not know. Othello enters and asks for the handkerchief because he has a cold, and Desdemona admits that she does not have it with her. Othello gets upset and berates her. Emilia suggests that he may be jealous, and Desdemona says she does not know him to be jealous. Iago and Cassio enter, and Cassio urges Desdemona to quicken his plea with Othello to which Desdemona replies that Othello is not himself and that Cassio should be patient. Iago then inquires about Othello and goes off to meet him. Desdemona imagines that something must be weighing on Othello to make him act the way he has, and believes that it is not her fault. She and Emilia go off to find Othello so that Desdemona can plead his case. Bianca enters and wants to know why Cassio has not seen her for a week, and he tells her that he has some pressing issues. He gives her the handkerchief, and she accuses him of getting it from another woman. He tells her he found it in his chamber and would like her to copy the design.

Analysis

The clown, who is Othello's servant, in this scene provides some comic relief to offset the intensity of the previous scene. When Desdemona asks him if he knows "where Lieutenant Cassio lies" he responds by saying "I dare not say he lies anywhere...He's a soldier; and for one to say a soldier lies is stabbing." The pun on the word *lie* is made when Desdemona asks for Cassio's whereabouts, but the clown responds as if she had called him a liar. The dramatic irony with this pun is clear because Iago's whole scheme is based on the lie of Desdemona's infidelity.

Othello enters and asks for the handkerchief. The significance of the handkerchief to Othello becomes clear because he talks

about how it was given to his mother by an Egyptian who "was a charmer and could read / The thoughts of people." He adds that there is "magic in the web of it." Othello's comments point out his susceptibility to the suggestion of charms and spells as a cultural trait, and makes Iago's manipulation of Othello more devious because he plays on Othello's vulnerability. The possible loss of the handkerchief infuriates Othello because, according to the spell woven in it, "To lose't or give't away wer such perdition / As nothing else could match." His strong reaction prompts Emilia to ask Desdemona if he were jealous to which Desdemona responds that she "ne'er saw this before." Emilia's subsequent comment that jealousy is "a monster / Begot upon itself, born on itself" echoes Iago's previous warning to Othello. However, Emilia is not motivated out of evil, but rather genuine concern for Desdemona. The incident is also a prelude to more of the behavior which is being manipulated by Iago. Desdemona is innocent of all deceit, so it is not surprising that she would believe Othello's change is caused by "something...of state / Either from Venice or some unhatched practice...in Cyprus."

When Iago and Cassio enter, Cassio asks Desdemona to hurry with her plea to Othello, and she says she will do what she can. Desdemona is not aware that this action will fulfill Iago's admonition to Othello in the previous scene to "Note if your lady strains his entertainment / With any stronger or vehement importunity."

At the end of the scene, the handkerchief becomes more significant because Cassio gives it to Bianca for her to copy its design. Iago's attempt to plant it in Cassio's lodging was successful, and Cassio inadvertently becomes trapped in the plot.

Study Questions

1. What function do the musicians and clown serve?

2. How does Iago's duplicity become evident when he speaks to Cassio?

3. What does Emilia's remark about the rift between Othello and Cassio suggest about their relationship?

4. Identify and explain two examples of irony found in Act III, Scene 3.

5. Explain how Iago manages to arouse Othello's suspicion in the conversation between Cassio and Desdemona.

6. How does Iago use Othello's racial differences against him?

7. How is the dropping of the handkerchief ironic?

8. What literary device is used to ease some of the dramatic tension that has been established?

9. How is the conversation about jealousy between Emilia and Desdemona ironic?

10. Explain the significance of the handkerchief to Othello.

Answers

1. The musicians and the clown serve as comic relief after the dramatic events of Act II. The musicians' serenade depicts an Elizabethan custom of awakening people of rank with music on special occasions. The clown's comment on the musicians' instruments provides bawdy humor for the audience and commentary on the health conditions of sixteenth century Naples.

2. Iago pretends to be acting on Iago's behalf when he tells him he will keep Othello away while Cassio and Desdemona speak. His real motive is to set up the circumstance in which Othello can find Cassio and Desdemona together for Iago to use as additional "ocular proof" of their infidelity.

3. When Emilia says that Iago is as upset by the rift between Cassio and Othello "as if the cause were his" she demonstrates how she too has been fooled by Iago's pretense. Emilia is also unaware that Iago is not what he presents himself to be.

4. Dramatic irony in which characters are not aware of the full impact of their words can be found in Emilia's statement that Iago is as upset as if he were the cause of the rift between Othello and him. She lacks the awareness that Iago did in fact instigate Roderigo to provoke the incident leading to Cassio's dismissal. In addition, Desdemona's statement

"that's an honest fellow," points out her lack of awareness that Iago is anything but honest.

5. Through a series of thoughts in half statements, innuendos, and facial gestures, Iago prompts Othello to think that Iago knows more than he is saying. As a result, Othello asks him to reveal his thoughts as vile as they may be. This is exactly what Iago wants in order to win Othello's trust even more.

6. First Iago points out that Othello's exotic nature isolates him from knowing Venetian culture as well as he himself does. He tells Othello that Venetian women are deceptive and uses Desdemona's elopement to support the fact that "she did deceive her father marrying you." He also plays upon Othello's cultural belief in magic when he reminds Othello that Brabantio thought his daughter was bewitched or she would never have forsaken all for Othello.

7. Irony of situation involves the occurrence of events that are opposite of the expectation of the character, audience, or reader. When Emilia picks up the handkerchief after it falls, Iago snatches it quickly when he comes in. This unforeseen event provides Iago with the object needed to eliminate Othello's uncertainty regarding Desdemona's infidelity with Cassio.

8. The pun, which depends on the multiple meanings of words, is used to create comic relief in the discussion between Desdemona and the clown. The word *lie* is used by Desdemona to ask where Cassio lodges, but the clown responds as if she were calling Cassio a liar. The comic use of the pun is also ironic because Iago's whole scheme depends on the many lies he tells.

9. Their conversation about jealousy is ironic because it follows Iago's attempts to provoke that emotion in Othello. It is also ironic because neither of them is aware of the depth to which Iago has played upon that emotion with Othello.

10. The handkerchief was given to him by his dying mother who instructed him to give it to his wife. Othello believes that the handkerchief is imbued with special powers to insure a

happy marriage. The loss of the handkerchief "were such perdition / As nothing could match." This belief becomes an obsession with Othello when he learns that Cassio has it, and the handkerchief becomes the object of his undoing.

Suggested Essay Topics

1. Identify characters and incidents which provide comic relief as the drama intensifies.

2. Trace the significance of Desdemona's handkerchief through Act III.

Act IV

Act IV, Scene 1

New Character:

Lodovico: *a Venetian nobleman, kinsman to Brabantio*

Summary

Before Othello's castle, Iago presents images of Desdemona's infidelity to Othello until he is overcome with emotion and falls into a trance. Cassio enters and asks what is wrong. Iago tells him that Othello has fallen into a fit of epilepsy and will speak to him later. Othello revives, and Iago tells him that Cassio came but will return. Moreover, he tells Othello to hide himself and watch Cassio's gestures as Iago speaks to him. When Cassio returns, Iago engages him in a conversation about Bianca, but Othello believes Cassio to be speaking about Desdemona and becomes furious. Bianca then enters complaining about the handkerchief he gave her to copy. Othello is convinced that Desdemona has been unfaithful and vows revenge. A trumpet announces the arrival of Lodovico, a Venetian nobleman, who brings letters from the Duke of Venice instructing Othello to return and appointing Cassio in his place. Desdemona, who also arrived, is pleased at this, and an enraged Othello strikes her. Lodovico, surprised at the change in Othello, inquires as to its cause.

Analysis

Iago continues to play upon the jealousy that he has generated in Othello with images of "a kiss in private" and "to be naked with her friend in bed." He adds that giving away a handkerchief is a visible act and suggests that honor can be given away and not seen. This reminds Othello of what Iago had previously said and "would most gladly have forgot it!" Iago does not want him to forget it and intensifies the pressure by saying that Cassio said he did "lie...with her, on her; what you will." At this point Othello is so overcome with emotion that he falls into a trance and Iago triumphantly says, "Work on / My medicine work!" relishing what his evil has wrought upon Othello. When Cassio enters, Iago creates the occasion to set up another damaging situation. When Othello revives and Iago informs him that Cassio will return, he tells Othello to "encave yourself / And mark the fleers, the gibes, the notable scorns / That dwell in every region of his face" as he prepares Othello for deception once more. When Cassio returns, Iago talks about Bianca so that Othello can conclude that Cassio's disparaging remarks are about Desdemona. Ironically, what adds more credibility to this seeming love affair is when Bianca enters and berates Cassio for giving her "some minx's token" to copy. Othello believes this to be Desdemona's handkerchief, and his response is to "Hang her!...chop her into messes, and poison her" expressing the degree which his emotions have reached. However, Iago suggests that he "strangle her in bed, even the bed she hath contaminated," a suggestion which foreshadows the dramatic climax of the play.

The end of the scene establishes the overt changes in Othello that have occurred over a short period of time. When Desdemona learns that Othello is commissioned back to Venice and Michael Cassio has been appointed in his stead, she is happy for Michael, but Othello interprets her genuine feeling as proof of their love. He strikes her, and Lodovico questions, "Is this the noble Moor whom our full Senate / Call all in all sufficient? Is this the nature whom passion could not shake?" It is clear that the "pestilence" with which Iago has infected Othello has not only changed the way he thinks but also the way he acts.

Act IV, Scene 2

Summary

Within the castle, Othello asks Emilia if she ever heard or saw anything suspicious when Desdemona and Cassio were together. Emilia contends that Desdemona is honest, and Othello tells her to go get Desdemona. When Emilia exits, Othello says that Emilia cannot be taken at her word. When Emila and Desdemona enter, Othello calls Desdemona a whore, and she is confused at this accusation because she is innocent. She wants to know what could she have done to get him into such a state. Emilia re-enters and Desdemona asks her to go get Iago. Emilia returns with Iago, and Desdemona asks him what she could do to win back Othello's respect. He tells her that the cause is some business of the state. Next, Roderigo enters and tells Iago that he is tired of being put off by Iago's schemes for him to win Desdemona. Iago quickly enlists Roderigo in a further scheme to kill Cassio before Othello leaves Cyprus.

Analysis

Othello's suspicions about Cassio and Desdemona have been aroused to the point that he asks Emilia "You have seen nothing then?" When she says she has not, she also tells him that "if any wretch have put this in your head / Let heaven requite it with the serpent's curse!" Her statement is another example of irony because neither she nor Othello recognize how true her charge is. When Desdemona enters, and Othello accuses her of being a whore, she is taken aback and wonders why he is acting so belligerently. When she admits only innocence he says "I took you for that cunning whore of Venice / That married with Othello." This interaction between the two of them is a direct contrast to a previous scene in which they were both overjoyed at seeing each other on Cyprus. The conversation underscores the drastic change Othello has undergone with Iago's insidious plan, and it emphasizes the deterioration of his belief in her fidelity. Ironically, Emilia adds that she believes "some most villainous knave, / Some base notorious knave, some scurvy fellow" has affected Othello to which Iago tells her to watch her words. She uses as support for her belief that "some such

squire he was / That turned your wit the seamy side without / And made you to suspect me with the Moor." This comment alludes to Iago's suspicion in Act II, Scene 1 and suggests that Iago is determined to make Othello, who is not inherently jealous, as jealous as he himself is.

When Roderigo enters, he is impatient at being stalled by Iago's schemes for him to win Desdemona. He says that "the jewels you have had from me to deliver to Desdemona would half have corrupted a votarist." Iago swindled Roderigo out of his possessions to use as gifts which he never delivered to Desdemona. He placates Roderigo's anger with a scheme to remove Cassio by "knocking out his brains" before Othello leaves Cyprus to make Roderigo think that Cassio is the obstacle between Desdemona and him.

Act IV, Scene 3

Summary

In another room, Othello leads Lodovico from the castle and tells Desdemona to prepare for bed and dismiss Emilia because he will return shortly. Desdemona senses something awry and sings a "willow song" about forsaken love and death. This prompts Desdemona to ask Emilia if there really are women who deceive their husbands, and Emilia replies that there are no doubt some such women. Desdemona asks Emilia if she would betray her husband to which Emilia responds that she wouldn't for trivial gain but would to make him a king. Desdemona insists she would never betray Othello. Emilia proceeds to tell her that the reason women fall is that their husbands neglect and are insensitive to them.

Analysis

The dominant impression in this scene is one of foreboding and imminent disaster. As Othello leads Lodovico away, he tells Desdemona to "Get you to bed on th' instant. I will be returned forthwith. Dismiss your attendant." Othello wants Desdemona alone so he can carry out his revenge, and she obeys his directive. After Othello leaves, Desdemona says that she has been preoccupied with a "willow" song about her mother's maid "who was in

love; and he she loved proved mad / And did forsake her."
Desdemona sings this song which foreshadows her death. The song
then prompts Desdemona to ask Emilia if there are men who abuse
women and Emilia replies "there be some such, no question" which
is ironic because Emilia is not aware that Iago is abusing her. In a
discussion of what makes women betray their husbands, Emilia
presents her opinion that "I do think it is their husbands' faults / If
wives do fall...The ills we do, their ills instruct us so." Emilia's comment suggests men's treatment of women is responsible for the
success or failure of a relationship, an idea which echoes the spirit
of independence which Elizabeth I instilled in her people during
her reign.

Study Questions

1. How does Othello react to Iago's images of infidelity?
2. Why does Iago speak to Cassio about Bianca?
3. Explain how the handkerchief has increased in significance.
4. How has Othello changed up to this point in the play?
5. Explain the difference in the relationship between Desdemona and Othello compared to when they first arrived in
   Cyprus.
6. Why is Emilia's belief about what is causing Othello's behavior ironic?
7. What clue does Emilia offer about Iago's own jealousy?
8. Why is Roderigo annoyed at Iago?
9. What is the dramatic significance of the "willow" song?
10. To what does Emilia attribute the fact that women betray
    their husbands?

Answers

1. When Iago suggests that Desdemona and Cassio "kiss in
   private" and lie naked together, Othello falls into a trance.
2. Iago carefully contrives to have Othello eavesdrop on a
   conversation between Cassio and him. When Iago elicits

responses from Cassio about Bianca, Othello thinks he is speaking disparagingly about Desdemona. Iago does this to convince Othello more conclusively of their secret love.

3. When Bianca enters, she jealously berates Cassio for having given her "some minx's token" and instructs him to "give it to your hobbyhorse." Of course Othello believes the hobbyhorse to be Desdemona and is indeed convinced of the clandestine affair between the two.

4. Before Iago began to instill ideas into Othello's head, Othello did not suspect Desdemona of any wrongdoing. In fact, jealousy is not part of his inherent nature. Iago has so goaded him that he now talks of killing Desdemona for what he believes is an act of adultery.

5. When they first arrived in Cyprus, each was overjoyed to see the other, and they talked in terms of endearing love. After Iago's instigation, Othello became so unlike himself that he was easily angered and even struck Desdemona in the presence of Lodovico and others.

6. Emilia affirms Desdemona's innocence to Othello and tells him to remove any thoughts of her infidelity "if any wretch have put this in your head." This is ironic because the very cause she suggests for his behavior is the truth. What makes this even more ironic is the fact that the "wretch" she speaks about is her husband.

7. When Emilia suggests that "some eternal villain, / Some busy and insinuatory rogue" devised a plot, Iago tells her "Fie there is no such man!" She continues, and he tells her to keep quiet. However, she alludes to "some such squire he was / That turned your wit the seamy side without / And make you to suspect me with the Moor."

8. He is tired of being promised access to Desdemona and never receiving it at Iago's whims. Iago has solicited jewels from Roderigo promising to give them to Desdemona as gifts. Consequently, Roderigo threatens to ask for the jewels back, give up his pursuit, and confess the scheme.

9. The melancholy nature of the song foreshadows the final scene of the play, and it creates an atmosphere of foreboding.

10. Emilia believes that when men "slack their duties / ...pour our treasures into foreign laps; / ...break out in peevish jealousies" they don't think that women are capable of resentment and have feelings. Therefore, women are pushed to the point of betrayal by their own husbands' insensitivities to them.

Suggested Essay Topics

1. Describe the changes that occur in Othello during the course of Act IV as Iago increases his attempts to rouse Othello's jealousy.

2. Defend or refute this statement: Emilia's opinion about betrayal expresses a contemporary view of the relationship between the sexes.

Act V

Act V, Scene 1

New Character:

Gratiano: *Venetian nobleman; brother to Brabantio*

Summary

On a street in Cyprus, Iago tells Roderigo to hide and attack Cassio as he walks by. However, when Cassio enters, Roderigo's attempt fails, and Cassio wounds him. Iago sneaks up behind Cassio and stabs him in the leg. Othello enters, hears Cassio's cries, and concludes that Iago has kept his word and killed Cassio. Lodovico and Gratiano enter at the confusion and comment on the cries for help coming from the street. Iago appears and asks them who is crying for help. Cassio then appears, is recognized, and says that whoever stabbed him is in the area. Roderigo cries for help and Iago immediately stabs him to death.

Bianca then enters the disturbance, and Iago suggests that she is part of the plot. Iago calls for a litter to bear off the dead Roderigo and wounded Cassio. Emilia now enters and wants to know what has just happened. Iago tells her that Cassio was attacked by Roderigo and others who escaped. He comments that this is the consequence of whoring. Next, he asks Emilia to find out where Cassio dined that evening. When Bianca admits that he was with her, Iago says that she will have some explaining to do.

Analysis

The opening of this scene provides the action to which all of Iago's scheming has been a prelude. Iago physically sets Roderigo in a position "behind this bulk" to attack Cassio, and he promises to be nearby. In an aside he comments that he has "rubbed this young quat almost to the senses / And he grows angry" in a tone of contempt for Roderigo who he has manipulated all along. When Iago says "Now whether he kill Cassio, / Or Cassio kill him, or each do kill the other, / Every way makes my gain" he demonstrates how little he values human life and how self serving he is. Cassio enters and Roderigo's attempt to kill him fails, and Cassio in turn wounds Roderigo. Iago's subsequent wounding of Cassio leads Othello to believe that Iago kept his word in his vow to kill Cassio, so he calls him "brave ...honest ...and just." The irony of this statement is that Othello still doesn't see the evil in Iago. The melee is disturbing enough to bring out Lodovico and Gratiano who comment on the dangerousness of the situation. Iago appears and seems to show concern for Cassio's wound, and when Roderigo appears, Cassio stabs him. The others believe that Iago acts out of revenge for his friend, but Iago's true motive in killing Roderigo is that he served his purpose and would certainly tell all if he lived.

When Bianca comes to see what is going on, Iago implicates her in the plot to kill Cassio. His derogatory attitude is expressed when he says that he suspects "this trash / To be party to the injury." This is another attempt to divert any suspicion away from himself. In a further ruse to appear beyond reproach he conducts an investigation into Cassio's whereabouts and asks where Cassio had dined. Bianca asserts that he dined with her, and Cassio charges her to go with him. The events of this scene occur rapidly to bring the play to its final dramatic scene.

Act V, Scene 2

Summary

Othello enters his bedchamber and sees Desdemona sleeping. As he beholds her beauty, he almost changes his mind about killing her. He kisses her, and when she awakens, he asks her if she

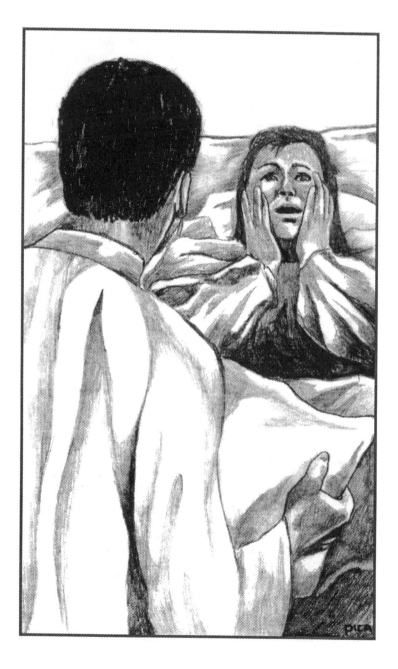

has prayed, accuses her of infidelity, and asks her about the handkerchief. She explains she never loved Cassio in the way Othello suggests, and she never gave him her handkerchief. Subsequently, Othello calls her a liar and says he saw Cassio with the handkerchief. Desdemona says that he must have found it, and Othello should ask him, to which Othello responds that Cassio is dead. When Desdemona expresses grief over this, Othello smothers her. Emilia enters with news that Cassio killed Roderigo. When Othello learns that Cassio is not dead, he realizes that something is not right. Desdemona cries out, dies, and Othello admits killing her. When Emilia asks why he killed her, Othello tells her to ask Iago about Desdemona's infidelity. Disbelieving Othello, Emilia cries out, and Montano, Gratiano, and Iago enter the bedchamber. Emilia asks Iago if he ever told Othello that Desdemona was unfaithful. When he admits that as the truth, Emilia calls him a liar and blames him for causing Othello to murder Desdemona. Iago charges her to get home, and she responds that she will obey him no longer. Gratiano says that Brabantio's death was fortunate, for to see Desdemona dead would surely kill him.

Othello says that he was sure of Desdemona's infidelity with Cassio and uses the handkerchief as proof. Emilia immediately responds by telling Othello that she gave the handkerchief to Iago who begged her to steal it. Othello runs at Iago, but Montano unarms him. Iago stabs Emilia and runs away. Montano and Gratiano chase after him. Lodovico and Montano enter with Cassio and Iago, and Othello wounds Iago with another sword he had in his chamber, but Othello is soon disarmed. Lodovico says that Iago confessed to his part in the attempt on Cassio's life and implicated Othello. Othello apologizes to Cassio who says he never gave Othello cause. Lodovico reveals that letters were found with Roderigo. Othello asks Cassio how he got the handkerchief, and Cassio says Iago planted it in his room. Lodovico discharges Othello and appoints Cassio in charge in Cyprus. Othello asks for a moment, stabs himself with a concealed weapon, falls across Desdemona, and dies.

Analysis

When Othello beholds "that whiter skin of hers than snow, / And smooth as monumental alabaster" he almost dismisses his suspicions of her. The image of the whiteness of her skin contrast with previous references to his blackness. His statement "Put out the light and then put out the light" suggests a comparison of the fragility of a candle flame to that of Desdemona's life. He admits that if he blows out a candle he can relight it, but if he kills her he cannot restore her life. This is a lucid moment amid the extremes of anger, jealousy, and rage which he has experienced in a short span of time. After he kisses her and she awakens, he is reminded of all that Iago has planted in his mind, and it is too late for him to reverse his course of action. In her fear, Desdemona asks for an explanation, and Othello says he saw Cassio with the handkerchief which Desdemona says she did not give to Cassio. Now he feels she is a liar, and with the news that Cassio is dead, Desdemona expresses grief. In a fit of jealous rage, he smothers her with a pillow.

When Emilia enters, a series of dialogue occur which unravels all the twisted elements of Iago's schemes. Othello expects "'Tis like she comes to speak of Cassio's death;" however, she asserts that "Cassio... hath killed a young Venetian / Called Roderigo" which prompts Othello to realize "Then murder's out of tune, / And sweet revenge grows harsh." This is the first sign that everything may not be as it seems.

Desdemona stirs, cries out, and dies. Consequently, Emilia calls Othello "the black devil" suggesting a contrast between the blackness of his deed to the whiteness of the slain Desdemona. Othello gives the reason that he killed her as "Cassio did top her. Ask thy husband." Here the imagery of sex is spoken of in animal terms, and it echoes Iago's first reference about Othello as "an old black ram tupping your white ewe" to Brabantio in the opening scene of Act I. Emilia, surprised that her husband would know this, calls for help.

When Iago comes in, Emilia confronts him with Othello's charge, and he admits that he did tell Othello. Emilia berates him, and he orders her to go home to which she replies "Perchance, Iago, I will ne'er go home."

We also learn of Brabantio's death from Gratiano, his brother, who says that "pure grief / shore his old thread in twain" after Desdemona left with Othello.

Obsessed with the handkerchief, Othello says that Desdemona gave it to Cassio as a token of her love. At this, Emilia immediately explains that it was she who gave it to Iago. Realizing for the first time that Iago tricked him, Othello charges at him with a sword, but Montano unarms him. To silence Emilia, Iago stabs her and runs out.

By this time Othello realizes that it is futile to attempt to escape his fate and is totally dishonored. When Lodovico enters after having apprehended Iago, he asks where Othello is, and he refers to himself as "he that was Othello." This perception suggests that he has already experienced a death and no longer exists. When Lodovico asks "Where is that viper," Othello remarks "If that thou be'st a devil, I cannot kill thee." For the first time the evil nature of Iago is recognized with references to him as a snake and a devil. After being wounded by Othello, Iago triumphantly replies, "I bleed, sir, but not killed."

Othello admits to his part in the plan to murder Cassio, and when Cassio says he gave Othello no cause, Othello asks his pardon. Othello realizes that he has been duped by Iago and wants to know why "that demi-devil / ...hath thus ensnared my soul and body." However he gets no explanation from Iago whose final comment is "From this time forth I never will speak word."

Lodovico discloses that letters found with Roderigo explain his attempt to kill Cassio, his discontent with Iago, and his upbraiding of Iago for making him provoke Cassio to a quarrel. Still unanswered for Othello is how Cassio came to possess the handkerchief. Cassio explains how he found it in his room and how Iago admitted putting it there "for a special purpose which wrought to his desire."

After all schemes are explained, Lodovico strips Othello of his command and appoints Cassio in charge. Othello's fate is to remain a closely guarded prisoner "Till that the nature of your fault be known / To the Venetian state."

Othello's final speech starkly contrasts his initial speech to the council. Othello who was once proud of his accomplishments yet humble in his presentation is now dishonored and humiliated with his last words. He is a man who has just experienced an agonizing personal defeat in contrast to his many glorious military triumphs. In just a short span of time he has been deceived by a man whom he trusted, sought the murder of his honorable lieutenant, and killed his faithful wife.

In his last words to everyone, Othello is concerned about how the events will be recorded. At first, he acknowledges that "he has done the state some service," but that is not his primary concern. He wants the truth about "these unlucky deeds" revealed without alteration. It is no surprise that he emphasizes truth after having been so maliciously deceived. Above all, he wants to be known as "one that loved not wisely, but too well." At this point Othello recognizes his love as a weakness because his misplaced love for Iago blinded him to Iago's treachery and to Desdemona's innocence. Othello faces the humiliation of "being wrought" by Iago's manipulation and "perplexed in the extreme." For Othello who has prided himself in his ability to use his mind in military service, manipulation is a devastating blow. In suggesting his own epitaph, Othello regrets having thrown "a pearl away / Richer than all his tribe." This metaphor compares Desdemona to a valuable precious stone which he threw away out of ignorance of its worth.

Othello shows remorse for his actions and, as one not given to a show of emotion, sheds "tears as fast as the Arabian trees / Their med'cinable gum." However, there is no medicine powerful enough to cure the ill. His final epithet of Iago as the "malignant and turbaned Turk" suggests that although Othello accepts responsibility for his crime, he realizes that he had been seduced by Iago's corruption. Othello's final description of himself as "the circumcised dog" suggests the level to which he has been reduced and evokes the animal imagery sustained throughout the play. At this point he draws a concealed weapon and kills himself rather than face dishonor. Lodovico's direct address to Iago as a "Spartan dog" is an apt label for "this hellish villain" who has succeeded in destroying all the goodness around him with his own malignancy.

Study Questions

1. Explain Iago's attitude toward Roderigo and Cassio.

2. How does Othello come to think that Cassio has kept his vow?

3. What function does the presence of Lodovico and Gratiano serve?

4. Why does Iago stab Roderigo?

5. How does Iago cast aside suspicion of his own part in the plot to kill Cassio?

6. When does Othello show a change of heart towards Desdemona?

7. Why does Othello mention the handkerchief so often?

8. Why does Othello kill Desdemona?

9. How are all the plots and schemes revealed at the end of the play?

10. Why does Othello kill himself?

Answers

1. Iago demonstrates a callous attitude toward Roderigo and Cassio. Up to this point he has used them to achieve his goals, so to him their deaths would be more valuable than their lives. If Roderigo is dead, then Iago would not have to compensate him for the jewels he tricked from him. If Cassio is dead, there is no risk of his being informed about Iago's plan by Othello.

2. When Othello hears Cassio cry out after being wounded by Iago, he believes that Iago has kept his vow to kill Cassio.

3. Lodovico and Gratiano enter the street at the cries for help. Lodovico's comment "Let's think't unsafe / To come into the cry without more help" suggests the danger that exists. Their presence also provides an "audience" for Iago's scenario to cast off all suspicion from himself.

4. Iago stabs Roderigo to unsure that he will not reveal any of Iago's scheming.

5. As soon as Bianca enters the confusion, Iago says, "I do suspect this trash / To be party in this injury." He uses Bianca as

a scapegoat to pretend that an investigation will reveal her complicity in the attempt to kill Cassio.

6. When Othello sees Desdemona sleeping, he begins to doubt his suspicions. The 'whiter skin of hers than snow / And smooth as alabaster tempt him to "not shed her blood."

7. The handkerchief was a significant gift from Othello's mother for what it represented and for the charms it supposedly held. It was the "ocular proof" he requested to believe Iago's accusation. Furthermore, his belief that Desdemona gave it away wounded him deeply and became an obsession because he never knew how Cassio really got the handkerchief until Cassio himself revealed the information.

8. Othello kills Desdemona because he is enraged by jealousy; he believes her to be a liar when she denies having given the handkerchief to Cassio; and she expresses grief at the news of Cassio's death.

9. At the end of the play Gratiano reveals that Brabantio has died. Othello learns that Emilia gave the handkerchief to Iago. Iago confesses his part in the plan to kill Cassio. Letters found with Roderigo reveal his part in the plan to eliminate Cassio. Another letter found on Roderigo reveals his discontent with Iago and his scheme to provoke Cassio to argument.

10. Othello kills himself because he recognizes the full weight of his crime. "He that was Othello" is already destroyed because he has lost honor, courage, and respect due to a "malignant and turbaned Turk." The disgrace of having all revealed would hurt more than his own suicide.

Suggested Essay Topics

1. Describe the rapid series of events which bring about Othello's demise.

2. Defend or refute this statement: Othello's suicide is an honorable act.

Sample Analytical Paper Topics

Topic #1

Generally, irony is the literary technique that involves differences between appearance and reality, expectation and result, or meaning and intention. More specifically, verbal irony uses words to suggest the opposite of what is meant. In dramatic irony there is a contradiction between what a character says or thinks and what the audience knows to be true. Finally situational irony refers to events that occur which contradict the expectations of the characters, audience, or readers. Identify the various types of irony used in *Othello* and explain their significance to the plot.

Outline

I.   Thesis Statement: *In Shakespeare's* Othello, *verbal irony, dramatic irony, and situational irony are used to propel the action forward and to intensify the drama as it proceeds.*

II. Act I

   A.   Iago tells Roderigo "I am not what I am."

   B.   Iago tells Othello "I lack iniquity / Sometimes to do me service."

   C.   Othello discusses how his merits will speak for themselves.

   D.   Brabantio wants Othello to go to prison for eloping with Desdemona.

    E. The invasion of Cyprus by the Turkish fleet causes Othello's commission to the island.

    F. Brabantio's insistence on how Desdemona was beguiled by Othello versus Iago's beguiling of Othello.

    G. Othello's comments to the Duke that Iago "is of honesty and trust"

III. Act II

    A. The storm destroys the Turkish fleet off the coast of Cyprus.

    B. In the humorous praise of women, Iago pretends that he has difficulty imagining ways to praise the various women Desdemona mentions.

    C. Othello tells Desdemona "If it were now to die, / 'Twere now to be most happy."

    D. Desdemona responds to Othello with "that our loves and comforts should increase / Even as our days grow!"

    E. Othello proclaims an evening of celebration of victory over the Turkish fleet and his marriage.

    F. Othello comments to Cassio, "Iago is most honest."

    G. Iago encourages Cassio to "have a measure to the health of black Othello."

    H. Iago tells Othello that he would "rather have his tongue cut" from his mouth "than it should do offense to Michael Cassio."

    I. Iago urges Cassio to ask Desdemona for help to get reinstated with Othello.

IV. Act III

    A. Iago tells Cassio that he will "devise a means to draw the Moor / Out of the way, that your converse and business / May be more free.

    B. Emilia says that the rift between Othello and Cassio "greives my husband / As if the cause were his."

C. Desdemona says to Cassio that "thy solicitor shall rather die / Than give thy cause away."

D. Iago says to Othello, "My lord, you know I love you."

E. Iago states to Othello that "men should be what they seem; / Or those that be not, would they might seem none!"

F. Othello comments that "This honest creature doubtless / Sees and knows more, much more, than he unfolds" with reference to Iago.

G. When Desdemona offers to bind Othello's head with her handkerchief, it falls and Emilia picks it up.

H. Othello tells Iago, "Thou hadst been better have been born a dog / Than answer my waked wrath" after demanding visible proof of Desdemona's infidelity.

I. Othello tells Desdemona that to lose or give away the handkerchief "were such perdition / As nothing else could match."

J. Cassio gives Bianca the handkerchief for her to copy the design.

V. Act IV

A. Iago instructs Othello to eavesdrop on a conversation he has with Cassio about Bianca.

B. Bianca enters and chides Cassio for giving her the handkerchief.

C. Lodovico delivers the letter recalling Othello to Venice and appointing Cassio in charge in Cyprus.

D. Emilia says to Othello that "If any wretch have put his in your head" to "Let heaven requite it with the serpent's curse."

E. Iago asks Desdemona "How comes this trick upon him?"

F. Emilia suggests that "some eternal villain ...devised the slander."

    G. Othello tells Desdemona to get "to bed on th' instant …dismiss your attendant there."

    H. Desdemona sings the "willow" song that preoccupied her mind all day.

VI. Act V

    A. Roderigo fails to kill Cassio

    B. Othello hears Cassio's cries.

    C. Iago kills Roderigo

    D. Bianca enters the fracas and wants to know what is going on.

    E. Iago tells Cassio "He that lies here…was my friend."

    F. Iago states that "guiltiness will speak, / Though tongues were out of use."

    G. Othello tells Desdemona that Cassio is dead.

    H. Emilia tells Othello that Cassio killed Roderigo.

    I. Iago's final statement is "From this time forth I never will speak word."

Topic #2

In literature, motivation refers to the reasons that explain or partially explain a character's thoughts, feelings, actions, or behavior. Motivation results from a combination of personality and circumstances with which he or she must deal. Samuel Taylor Coleridge describes the character of Iago in Shakespeare's *Othello* as a "motiveless malignancy," suggesting that he is a character whose motivation is pure evil. Discuss Iago in terms of the thoughts, feelings, actions, and behavior which result from his experiences.

Outline

I.   Thesis Statement: *Iago is a manifestation of evil from which emanates a malevolent force that grows wider and deeper, destroying everyone in its path as he reveals himself throughout the play.*

II. Act I

    A. Roderigo responds to Iago with "Thou told'st me thou didst hold him in thy hate."

    B. Iago expresses his opinions as to why Michael Cassio was chosen as Othello's lieutenant.

    C. Iago comments that "In following him, I follow but myself."

    D. Iago urges Roderigo to awaken Brabantio with news of the elopement.

    E. Iago presents images of animal lust to Brabantio.

    F. Iago does not reveal himself to Brabantio.

    G. Iago tells Othello how he had to defend Othello to Brabantio many times.

    H. Roderigo threatens to drown himself, but Iago consoles him with promises of Desdemona.

    I. Iago tells Roderigo, "Let's be conjunctive in our revenge."

III. Act II

    A. Iago insists that it is difficult for him to easily imagine the praises for women that Desdemona asks.

    B. Iago carefully observes Michael Cassio's greeting of Desdemona.

    C. Iago reveals in an aside that he will "untune" Desdemona and Othello.

    D. Iago informs Roderigo of the greeting which Michael Cassio gave to Desdemona.

    E. Iago enlists Roderigo in a plan to anger Cassio and provoke him to a quarrel.

    F. Iago admits that he suspects Othello of infidelity with Emilia

    G. Iago tells Cassio that Othello relieved them from the watch.

- H. Iago insists on toasting to Othello with Cassio.

- I. Iago informs Montano that Cassio's weakness is drinking.

- J. Iago instigates Roderigo to provoke a quarrel with Cassio.

- K. Othello hears Iago's version of the scuffle.

- L. Iago urges Cassio to ask Desdemona for help.

IV. Act III

- A. Iago tells Cassio he will keep Othello away as Michael Cassio speaks with Desdemona.

- B. Iago engages in conversation with Othello regarding his thoughts.

- C. Iago plants thoughts of jealousy in Othello's mind regarding Cassio and Desdemona.

- D. Iago snatches the handkerchief from Emilia.

- E. Iago tells Othello he has seen Cassio with the handkerchief.

- F. Iago promises to follow through with Othello's vow for revenge.

V. Act IV

- A. Iago feeds Othello with images of lust and love between Cassio and Desdemona.

- B. Iago schemes to have Othello overhear a conversation he has with Bianca.

- C. Iago encourages close observation of Othello's behavior after he strikes Desdemona.

- D. Iago suggests to Desdemona that Othello's behavior is "but his humour."

- E. After Roderigo expresses impatience with Iago, he suggests that Rogerigo get involved in the plan to eliminate Michael Cassio by "knocking out his brains."

VI. Act V

    A.   Iago expresses his attitude toward Cassio's and Roderigo's lives.

    B.   In the scuffle between Cassio and Roderigo, Iago wounds Cassio.

    C.   Iago cries for help for Cassio after Lodovico and Gratiano come onto the scene.

    D.   Iago pretends to search for those responsible for the villainy.

    E.   Iago kills Roderigo.

    F.   Bianca is implicated in a plot to kill Cassio.

    G.   Iago states he will speak no more.

Topic #3

Othello is a play in which many contrasts affect the characters' ability to discern the difference between reality and illusion. Identify and trace the contrasts between black and white images, love and lost, and honesty and dishonesty as they are presented throughout the play.

Outline

I. Thesis Statement: *The juxtaposition of images of dark and light, love and lust, and honesty and dishonesty clouds the characters' perception so much so that they are unable to distinguish the difference between reality and illusion.*

II. Light and dark

    A.   Roderigo refers to Othello as "the thick-lips."

    B.   Roderigo awakens Brabantio at night, and Brabantio demands light to seek Desdemona.

    C.   Iago suggests that Cassio drink a measure to "the black Othello."

    D.   Othello refers to Desdemona's "whiter skin …than snow / And smooth as monumental alabaster."

    E.   Othello comments "Put out the light, and then put out the light!"

III. Love and lust

    A.   Iago comments to Brabantio that he'll have his daughter "covered with a Barbary horse...[his] nephews neigh to [him] and coursers for cousins, and gennets for germans."

    B.   Iago refers to Othello and Desdemona as "making the beast with two backs" with reference to the consumation of their marriage.

    C.   Iago tells Roderigo that when Desdemona's appetite for Othello fades she will desire Cassio.

    D.   Iago fills Othello's mind with various images of animal acts of copulation to rouse his jealousy.

    E.   Othello tells Emilia he killed his wife because "Cassio did top her."

    F.   Desdemona and Othello speak in terms of deep love when they meet in Cyprus.

IV. Honesty and dishonesty

    A.   Iago reveals to Roderigo "I am not what I am."

    B.   Iago tells Othello that he has defended him to Brabantio many times.

    C.   Roderigo is tricked into thinking that all of Iago's plans for him will get him to Desdemona.

    D.   Desdemona believes Iago to be an honest man.

    E.   Iago tells Cassio to plead his case with Desdemona.

    F.   Iago tells Othello to eavesdrop on a conversation he has with Cassio.

SECTION EIGHT

Bibliography

Othello. The Folger Library. Wright, Louis B. and Virginia A. Lamar, Eds. New York: Washington Square Press, 1957.

Shakespearean Criticism. Mark Scott, Ed. Detroit, Michigan: Gale Research Company Book Tower, 1987.

Speaight, Robert. *Shakespeare on The Stage*. Boston and Toronto: Little, Brown and Company, 1973.